The Cambridge Manuals of Science and
Literature

NAVAL WARFARE

T0345955

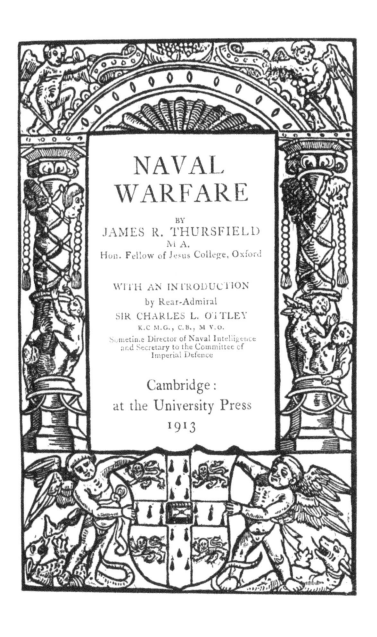

NAVAL WARFARE

BY

JAMES R. THURSFIELD
M.A.
Hon. Fellow of Jesus College, Oxford

WITH AN INTRODUCTION
by Rear-Admiral
SIR CHARLES L. OTTLEY
K.C.M.G., C.B., M.V.O.
Sometime Director of Naval Intelligence
and Secretary to the Committee of
Imperial Defence

Cambridge:
at the University Press
1913

CAMBRIDGE UNIVERSITY PRESS
Cambridge, New York, Melbourne, Madrid, Cape Town,
Singapore, São Paulo, Delhi, Tokyo, Mexico City

Cambridge University Press
The Edinburgh Building, Cambridge CB2 8RU, UK

Published in the United States of America by Cambridge University Press, New York

www.cambridge.org
Information on this title: www.cambridge.org/9781107605756

© Cambridge University Press 1913

First published 1913
First paperback edition 2011

A catalogue record for this publication is available from the British Library

ISBN 978-1-107-60575-6 Paperback

*With the exception of the coat of arms at
the foot, the design on the title page is a
reproduction of one used by the earliest known
Cambridge printer, John Siberch,* 1521

CHAPTER VI

ENGLAND has not been invaded since A.D. 1066, when, the country having no fleet in being, William the Conqueror effected a landing and subjugated the kingdom. During the eight centuries and more that have since elapsed, every country in Europe has been invaded and its capital occupied, in many cases more than once. It is by no means for lack of attempts to invade her that England has been spared the calamity of invasion for more than eight hundred years. It is not because she has had at all times— it may indeed be doubted if she has had at any time —organized military force sufficient to repel an invader, if he could not be stopped at sea. It is because she can only be invaded across the sea, and because whenever the attempt has been made she has always had naval force sufficient to bring the enterprise to nought. It is merely a truism to say that the invasion of hostile territory across the sea is a much more difficult and hazardous enterprise than the crossing of a land frontier by organized military force. But it is no truism to say that the reason why it is so much more difficult and more

INTRODUCTION

THE title chosen by its author for this little volume would assuredly commend it to the Naval Service, even if that author's name were not—as it is—a household word with more than one generation of naval officers. But to such of the general public as are not yet familiar with Mr Thursfield's writings a brief word of introduction may perhaps be useful. For the matters herein dealt with are by no means of interest only to the naval profession. They have their bearing also on every calling and trade. In these days when national policy is at the mercy of the ballot-box, it is not too much to say that a right understanding of the principles of maritime warfare is almost as desirable amongst civilians as amongst professional sailors.

Regrettable indeed would it be if the mere fact that this little book bears a more or less technical title should tempt the careless to skip its pages or pitch it to that dreary limbo which attends even the best of text-books on subjects which we think do not concern us. The fruits of naval victory, the calamities attendant on naval defeat are matters

which will come home—in Bacon's classic phrase—
to the business and the bosoms of all of us, landsmen
and seamen alike. Most Englishmen are at least
dimly aware of this. They realise, more or less re-
luctantly perhaps, that a decisive British defeat at
sea under modern conditions would involve unspeak-
able consequences, consequences not merely fatal to
the structure of the Empire but destructive also
of the roots of our national life and of the well-
being of almost all individuals in these islands.

Elementary prudence insists on adequate safeguards against evils so supreme, and amongst
those safeguards the education of the people to-day
occupies a foremost place. Our Empire's destinies
for good and evil are now in the hands of the masses
of the people. Sincerely as all lovers of ordered
freedom may rejoice in this devolution of political
power to the people, thoughtful men will be apt
to reflect that an uninstructed crowd is seldom
right in its collective action. If Ministerial responsibility has dwindled, *pro tanto* that of each
one of His Majesty's lieges has enormously increased ; and it is more incumbent on the nation's
rank and file to-day than ever in the past to equip
themselves with the knowledge necessary to enable
them to record their votes aright.

It is from this point of view that this Manual
should be read. It epitomises the principles upon

which success in naval warfare depends. It shows how the moral factor in all cases and at every epoch dominates and controls the material ; how the "*animus pugnandi*," as Mr Thursfield calls it, the desire to get at the enemy in "anything that floats," transcends every other weapon in a nation's armoury ; how if that spirit is present, all other difficulties can be surmounted, and how without it the thickest armour, the biggest all-shattering guns shrivel in battle to the measure of mere useless scrap iron.

This is the message of the book for the seaman. But—and this is of the essence of the whole matter —for the landsman it has also a lesson of a very different kind. His responsibility is for the material factor in naval war. Let him note the supreme value of the moral factor ; let him encourage it with all possible honour and homage, but let him not limit his contribution to the nation's fighting capital to any mere empty lip-service of this kind. The moral factor is primarily the sailor's business. The landsman's duty is to see to it that when war comes our sailors are sent to sea, not in "anything that floats" but in the most modern and perfect types of warship that human ingenuity can design.

How can this fundamental duty be brought home to the individual Englishman ? Certainly not by asking him to master the niceties of modern naval technique, matters on which every nation must trust to its experts. But, the broad principles of naval warfare are to-day precisely as they were at Salamis or Lepanto; and to a people such as ours, whose history from its dawn has been moulded by maritime conditions, and which to-day more than ever depends upon free oversea communications for its continued existence, these broad principles governing naval warfare have so real a significance that they may wisely be studied by all classes of the community.

Tactics indeed have profoundly altered, and from age to age may be expected to change indefinitely. But so long as the sea remains naval warfare will turn upon the command of the sea; a " Fleet in Being " will not cease to be as real a threat to its foe as it was in the days of Torrington; invasion of oversea territory will always be limited by the same inexorable factors which for centuries have told in favour of the British race and have kept the fields of England inviolate from the tread of a conqueror.

There are indications that still more heavy sacrifices will be demanded from the British tax-payer for the upkeep of the Fleet in the future than has been the case even in the recent past. Nothing but iron necessity can justify this unfruitful expenditure, this alienation of the national resources in men and money to the purposes of destruction. Even as it is, naval administrators are finding it increasingly difficult to carry all sections of politicians and the whole of the masses of this country with them in these ever-increasing demands. The best way of ensuring that future generations of Englishmen will rise to the necessary height of a patriotic sense of duty and will record their votes in support of such reasonable demands is to prepare their minds by an elementary knowledge of what naval warfare really means.

No Englishman, so far as the writer is aware, is better fitted than Mr Thursfield to undertake this task, and this little book is a very excellent example of the way in which that task should be fulfilled. It unites—very necessarily—a high degree of condensation with a simplicity of language and a lucidity of exposition both alike admirable. And Mr Thursfield's right to be heard on naval questions is second to that of no civilian in these islands. His relations with the British Navy have been for more than a quarter of a century of the closest kind. His reputation in the particular field of literary endeavour which he has made his own ranks high amongst writers as celebrated as Admiral Mahan, Sir George Sydenham Clarke (Lord Sydenham), the late Sir John Colomb, and his brother the late Admiral P. H. Colomb, Sir

J. K. Laughton, Admiral Sir Cyprian Bridge, Admiral Sir R. N. Custance, Mr Julian Corbett, Mr David Hannay, Mr Archibald Hurd, and others. In the domain of naval history, its philosophy and its literature, he has done brilliant work. When it is added that Mr Thursfield is known to have been, for many years, one of the chief naval advisers of *The Times*, enough will probably have been said to ensure a sympathetic attention for this the veteran author's latest publication.

C. L. OTTLEY

24th July 1913

PREFACE

INTELLIGENT readers of this little Manual will perceive at once that it pretends to be nothing more than an introduction, quite elementary in character, to the study of naval warfare, its history, and its principles as displayed in its history. As such, I trust it may be found useful by those of my countrymen who desire to approach the naval problems which are constantly being brought to their notice and consideration with sound judgment and an intelligent grasp of the principles involved in their solution. It is the result of much study and of a sustained intimacy with the sea service, both afloat and ashore, such as few civilians have been privileged to enjoy in greater measure. Even so, I should have thought it right, as a civilian, to offer some apology for undertaking to deal with so highly technical and professional a subject, were I not happily relieved of that obligation by the kindness of my friend Rear-Admiral Sir Charles L. Ottley, who has, at the instance of the Editors of this series, contributed to this volume an Introduction in which my qualifications are set forth with an appreciation which I cannot but regard as far too flattering. It would ill become me to add a single word—unless it were of deprecation—to credentials expounded on such high authority.

I should hope that readers who have found this volume useful to them will not confine their studies to it. Abundant materials for a deeper and more comprehensive study of the subject will be found in the several works incidentally mentioned or quoted in my text, and in the writings of those other contemporary authors with whom Sir Charles Ottley has done me the high honour to associate myself. In these several works further guidance to a still more sustained study of the subject will be found, and in this regard I would specially mention the admirable *Short History of the Royal Navy*, by Mr David Hannay—two volumes which, in addition to their other and more conspicuous merits, contain a well-selected list of authorities to be consulted prefixed to each chapter. These references, which in truth cover the whole subject, will, I trust, better serve the purpose of the advanced or advancing student than any such Bibliography as I could compile on a scale commensurate with the form and purpose of the present Manual.

Readers of my other writings on naval topics will, perhaps, observe that in one or two cases, where the same topics had to be discussed, I have

not hesitated to reproduce, with or without modifica-
tion, the language I had previously employed.
This has been done deliberately. The topics so
treated fell naturally and, indeed, necessarily within
the scope of the present volume. To exclude them
because I had discussed them elsewhere was impossible. Wherever I found I could improve the
language previously employed in the direction of
greater lucidity and precision I have done so to
the best of my ability, so that the passages in
question are close paraphrases rather than mere
transcripts of those which occur elsewhere. But I
have not attempted to disguise or weaken by para-
phrase any passages which still seemed to me to
convey my meaning better than any other words I
could choose.

Changes in the methods, though not in the principles, of naval warfare are in these days so rapid
and often so sudden that one or two topics have
emerged into public prominence even since the
present volume was in type. I desire therefore
to take this opportunity of adding a few supple-
mentary remarks on them. The first, and possibly
in the long run the most far-reaching of these topics,
is that of aviation, which I have only mentioned
incidentally in the text. That aviation is still in
its infancy is a truism. But to forecast the scope
and direction of its evolution is as yet impossible.

For the moment it may perhaps be said that its offensive capacity—its capacity, that is, to determine or even materially to affect the larger issues of naval warfare—is inconsiderable. I say nothing of the future, whether immediate or remote. Any day may witness developments which will give entirely new aspects to the whole problem. In the meanwhile the chief functions of aircraft in war will probably be, for some time to come, those of scouting, observation, and the collection and transmission of intelligence not obtainable by any other means. Offensive functions of a more direct and formidable character will doubtless be developed in time, and may be developed soon ; but as I am no prophet I cannot attempt to forecast the direction of the evolution, to determine its limits, or to indicate its probable effects on the methods of naval warfare as expounded in the following pages. I will, however, advance two propositions which will not, I believe, be gainsaid by competent authorities. They are true for the moment, though how long they may remain true I do not know. One is that no aircraft yet constructed can take or keep the air in all conditions of weather. The number of days in the year in which it can do so in safety can only be represented by the formula $365 - x$, in which x is as yet an unknown quantity, though it is no doubt a quantity which will diminish as the art of aviation is developed. The other is that there is as yet no known method of navigating an aircraft with accuracy and precision out of sight of land. The air-currents by which it is affected are imperceptible to those embarked, variable and indeterminate in their force and direction, and quite incapable of being charted beforehand. In these conditions an airman who sought to steer by compass alone, say, from Bermuda to New York, might perchance find himself either at Halifax, on the one hand, or at Charleston on the other.

In my chapter on "Invasion" no mention is made of those subsidiary forms of military enterprise across the sea which are known as raids. I have treated invasion as an enterprise having for its object the subjugation of the country invaded, or at least the subjection of its people and their rulers to the enemy's will. As such it requires a force commensurate in numbers with the object to be attained, and it stands to reason that this force must needs be so large that its chances of evading the vigilance of an enemy who is in effective command of the sea must always be infinitesimal. A raid, on the other hand, is an enterprise of much lesser magnitude and much smaller moment. Its method is to elude the enemy's naval guard at this or that point of his territory; and, having done so, its

purpose is to land troops at some vulnerable point
of the territory assailed, there to create alarm and
confusion and to do as much harm as they can—
which may be considerable before their sea communications are severed by the defending naval force
assumed to be still in effective command of the sea
affected. If that command is maintained, the
troops engaged in the raid must inevitably be
reduced sooner or later to the condition of a forlorn
hope which has failed. If, on the other hand, that
command is overthrown, then the troops aforesaid
may prove to be the advanced guard of an invasion
to follow. Thus, although a successful raid may
sometimes be carried out in the teeth of an adverse
command of the sea, yet it cannot be converted
into an invasion until that adverse command has
been assailed and overthrown. It is thus essentially
fugitive in character, possibly very effective as a
diversion, certain to be mortifying to the belligerent
assailed, and not at all unlikely to cause him much
injury and even more alarm, but quite incapable
of deciding the larger issues of the conflict so long
as his command of the sea remains unchallenged.
It is perhaps expedient to say this much on the
subject, because the programme of the Naval
Manœuvres of this year is known to have included
a series of raids of this fugitive character. Whether,
or to what extent, any of these operations were

adjudged to have been successful I do not know.
I am only concerned to point out that, whether
successful or not, their utmost success can throw
little or no light on the problem of invasion unless
in the course of the same operations the defenders'
command of the sea was adjudged to have been
overthrown.

In my chapter on " The Differentiation of Naval
Force " I endeavoured to define the functions of the
so-called " battle-cruiser " and to forecast its special
uses in war. At the same time I pointed out that
" it is held by some high authorities that the battle-
cruiser is in very truth a hybrid and an anomaly, and
that no adequate reason for its existence can be
given." It would appear that the views of these
high authorities have now been adopted, in some
measure at least, by the Admiralty. Since the
chapter in question was in type it has been officially
announced that the battle-cruiser has been placed
in temporary, and perhaps permanent, abeyance.
Its place is to be taken by a special type of fast
battleship, vessels in every way fit to lie in a line
and yet, at the same time, endowed with qualities
which, without unduly increasing their size and
displacement, will enable them to discharge the
special functions which I assigned to the battle-
cruiser in the line of battle. This is done by
employing oil instead of coal as the source of the

ship's motive power. The change thus adumbrated would seem to be in the natural order of evolution, and at the same time to be in large measure one rather of nomenclature than of substance. The battle-cruiser, as its name implies, is itself essentially a fast battleship in one aspect and an exceedingly powerful cruiser in another. In the fast battleship which is to replace it, the battle function will be still further developed at the expense of the cruiser function. But its speed will still qualify it to be employed as a cruiser whenever occasion serves or necessity requires, just as the battle-cruiser was qualified to lie in a line and do its special work in a fleet action. The main difference is that the fast battleship is much less likely to be employed as a cruiser than the battle-cruiser was; but I pointed out in the text that the employment even of the battle-cruiser in cruiser functions proper was likely to be only occasional and subsidiary.

The decision to use oil as the exclusive source of the motive power of fast battleships, and of certain types of small cruisers of exceptional speed, is undoubtedly a very significant one. It may be taken to point to a time when oil only will be employed in the propulsion of warships and coal will be discarded altogether. But that consummation can only be reached when the internal combustion engine has been much more highly developed for

purposes of marine propulsion than it is at present.
At present oil is only employed in large warships
for the purpose of producing steam by the external
combustion of the oil. But it may be anticipated
that a process of evolution, now in its initial stages
in the Diesel and other internal combustion engines,
will in course of time result in the production of an
internal combustion engine capable of propelling the
largest ships at any speed that is now attainable by
existing methods. When that stage is reached oil
will, for economic reasons alone, undoubtedly hold
the field for all purposes of propulsion in warships.
It is held by some that this country will then be
placed at a great disadvantage, inasmuch as it
possesses a monopoly of the best steam coal, whereas
it has no monopoly of oil at all, and probably no
sufficient domestic supply of it to meet the needs of
the Fleet in time of war. But oil can be stored as
easily as coal and, unlike coal, it does not deteriorate
in storage. To bring it in sufficient supplies from
abroad in time of war should be no more difficult
for a Power which commands the sea than to bring
in the supplies of food and raw material on which
this country depends at all times for its very existence. Moreover, even if we continued to depend
on coal alone, that coal, together with other supplies
in large quantities, must, as I have shown in my
last chapter, be carried across the seas in a continuous

stream to our fleets in distant waters, and one of
the great advantages of oil over coal is that it can
be transferred with the greatest ease to the warships
requiring it at any rendezvous on the high seas,
whether in home waters or at the uttermost ends
of the globe, which may be most conveniently
situated for the conduct of the operations in hand.
For these reasons I hold that no serious apprehension
need be entertained lest the supply of oil to our
warships should fail so long as we hold the command
of the sea. If ever we lost the command of the
sea we should not be worrying about the supply of
oil. Oil or no oil, we should be starving, destitute
and defenceless.

It only remains for me to express my gratitude
to my friend Sir Charles Ottley, not merely for an
Introduction in which I cannot but fear that he
has allowed his friendship to get the better of his
judgment, but also for his kindness in devoting so
much of his scanty leisure to the reading of my
proofs and the making of many valuable suggestions
thereon. I have also to thank my friend Captain
Herbert W. Richmond, R.N., for his unselfish kindness in allowing me to make use of his notes on the
Dunkirk campaign which he has closely studied
in the original papers preserved at the Admiralty
and the Record Office. To my son, Lieutenant
H. G. Thursfield, R.N., I am also indebted for many

valuable suggestions. Finally, my acknowledgments are due to the Editors of this series and the Syndics of the Cambridge University Press for their uniform courtesy and consideration.

J. R. T.

4th September 1913.

NAVAL WARFARE

CHAPTER I

INTRODUCTORY

WAR is the armed conflict of national wills, an appeal to force as between nation and nation. Naval warfare is that part of the conflict which takes place on the seas. The civilized world is divided into separate, independent States or nations, each sovereign within its own borders. Each State pursues its own ideas and aims and embodies them in a national policy ; and so far as this policy affects only its own citizens, it is subject to no control except that of the national conscience and the national sense of the public welfare. Within the State itself civil war may arise when internal dissensions divide the nation into two parties, of which either pursues a policy to which the other refuses to submit. In this case, unless the two parties agree to separate without conflict, as was done by Sweden and Norway a few years ago, an armed conflict ensues and the nation is divided into two belligerent States which may or may not

A

become, according to the fortune of war, separate, independent, and sovereign in the end. The great example of this in our own time was the War of Secession in America, which, happily for both parties, ended without disruption, in the surrender of the weaker of the two, and after a time in a complete reconciliation between them.

Thus war may arise between two parties in a single State, and when it does the two parties become, to all intents and purposes, separate, independent, and sovereign States for the time being, and are, for the most part, so regarded and treated by other independent States not taking part in the conflict. For this reason, though the origin of a civil war may differ widely in all its circumstances and conditions from that of a war between two separate States, sovereign and independent *ab initio*, yet as soon as a state of war is established, as distinct from that of a puny revolt or a petty rebellion, there is, for a student of war, no practical difference between a civil war and any other kind of war. Both fall under the definition of war as the armed conflict of national wills.

Between two separate, sovereign, independent nations a state of war arises in this wise. We have seen that the internal policy of an independent State is subject to no direct external control. But States do not exist in isolation. Their citizens

trade with the citizens of other States, seeking to
exchange the products of their respective industries
to the advantage of both. As they grow in pros-
perity, wealth, and population, their capital seeks
employment in other lands, and their surplus
population seeks an outlet in such regions of the
earth as are open to their occupation. Thus arise
external relations between one State and another,
and the interests affected by these relations are
often found—and perhaps still more often believed
—by one State to be at variance with those of
another. In pursuit of these interests—which, as
they grow and expand, become embodied in great
consolidated kingdoms, great colonial empires, or
great imperial dependencies, and tend to be regarded
in time as paramount to all other national interests
—each State formulates and pursues an external
policy of its own which may or may not be capable
of amicable adjustment to the policy of other
States engaged in similar enterprises. It is the
function of diplomacy to effect adjustments such
as these where it can. It succeeds much more often
than it fails. Conflicting policies are deflected by
mutual agreement and concession so as to avoid
the risk of collision, and each State, without aban-
doning its policy, modifies it and adjusts it to the
exigencies of the occasion. Sometimes, however,
diplomacy fails, either because the conflicting

policies are really irreconcilable, or because passion, prejudice, national ambition, or international misunderstanding induces the citizens of both States and their rulers so to regard them. In that case, if neither State is prepared so to deflect its policy as to avert collision, war ensues. The policy remains unchanged, but the means of further pursuing it, otherwise than by an appeal to force, are exhausted. War is thus, according to the famous definition of Clausewitz, the pursuit of national policy by other means than those which mere diplomacy has at its command—in other words by the conflict of armed force. Each State now seeks to bend its enemy's will to its own and to impose its policy upon him.

The means of pursuing this policy vary almost indefinitely. But inasmuch as war is essentially the conflict of armed force, the primary object of each belligerent must in all cases be to subdue, and, in the last resort, to destroy the armed forces of the adversary. When that is done all is done that war can do. How to do this most speedily and most effectively is the fundamental problem of war. There is no cut-and-dried solution of the problem, because although war may be considered, as it has been considered above, in the abstract, it is the most concrete of all human arts and, subject to the fundamental principle above enunciated, its particular forms may, and indeed must, vary with the circumstances and conditions of each particular war. Many commentators on war distinguishing, with Clausewitz, between " limited " and " unlimited " war, would further insist that the forms of war must vary with its objects. I cannot follow this distinction, which seems to me to be inconsistent with the fundamental proposition of Clausewitz, to the effect that war is the pursuit of policy by means of the conflict of armed force. If you desire your policy to prevail you must take the best means that are open to you to make it prevail. It is worse than useless to dissipate your energies in the pursuit of any purpose, however important in itself, which does not directly conduce, and conduce better than any other purpose you could pursue, to that paramount end. The only limitation of your efforts that you can tolerate is that they should involve the least expenditure of energy that may be necessary to make your policy prevail. But that is a question of the economics of war ; it is not a question of " limited war " or of " war for a limited object." Your sole object is to bend the enemy to your will. That object is essentially an unlimited one, or one that is limited only by the extent of the efforts which the enemy makes to withstand you. The only sure way of attaining this object is to destroy his armed forces. If he submits before this is done it is he that limits the war, not you. Bacon's unimpeachable maxim in this regard is often misinterpreted. "This much is certain," he says, "he that commands the sea is at great liberty and may take as much or as little of the war as he will." That is indisputable, but its postulate is that the belligerent has secured the command of the sea ; that is, as I shall show hereafter, that he has subdued, if not destroyed, the armed forces of the enemy afloat. Having done that he may, in a certain sense, take as much or as little of the war as he chooses ; but he must always take as much as will compel the enemy to come to terms.

Naval warfare is no essential part of the armed conflict between contending States. In some cases it exercises a decisive influence on the conduct and issue of the conflict, in others none at all or next to none. But sea power, that is, the advantage which a nation at war derives from its superiority at sea, may largely affect the issue of a war, even though no naval engagements of any moment may take place. In the Crimean War the unchallenged supremacy of England and France on the seas alone made it possible for the Allies to invade the Crimea and undertake the siege of Sebastopol ; while the naval campaigns of the Allies in the Baltic, although they resulted in no decisive naval operation, yet largely contributed to the success of the Allied arms

in the Crimea by compelling Russia to keep in the
north large bodies of troops which might otherwise
have turned the scale against the Allies in the South.
In the War of 1859, between France and Austria,
with the Sardinian kingdom allied to the former,
the superiority of the Allies at sea enabled considerable portions of the French army to be transported
from French to Piedmontese ports, and by threaten-
ing the flank of the Austrian line of advance, it
accelerated the concentration of the Allies on the
Ticino. It also enabled the Allies to maintain a
close blockade of the Austrian ports in the Adriatic,
and might have led to an attack from the sea on the
Austrian rear in Venetia had not the military
reverses of Austria in Lombardy brought the war
to an end. In the War of Secession in America
the issue was largely determined, or at least accelerated, by the close but not impenetrable blockade
established by the North over the ports and coasts
of the South, and by the co-operation of Farragut
on the Mississippi with the Federal land forces
in that region. On the other hand, in the War of
1866 there was no naval conflict worth mentioning
between Austria and Prussia, because Prussia had
no navy to speak of ; but as Italy, a naval Power,
was the ally of Prussia, and as Austria had a small
but very efficient naval force led by a great naval
commander, the conflict between these two Powers

led to the Battle of Lissa, in which the Italian fleet was decisively defeated, though the triumph of Prussia over the armies of Austria saved Italy from the worst consequences of defeat, and indeed obtained for her, in spite of her military reverses on land, the coveted possession of Venetia. In the War of 1870 again, although the supremacy of France on the seas was never seriously challenged by Prussia, yet her collapse on land was so sudden and complete that her superiority at sea availed her little or nothing. The maritime trade of Prussia was annihilated for the time, but it was then too insignificant a factor in the economic fabric of Prussia for its destruction to count for much, and the fleets of France rode triumphant in the North Sea and the Baltic; but finding no ships to fight, having no troops to land, and giving a wide berth to fortifications with which they were ill-equipped— as ships always are and always must be—to contend without support from the military arm, their presence was little more than an idle and futile demonstration. In the Boer War the influence of England's unchallenged supremacy at sea, albeit latent, was decisive. The Boers had no naval force of any kind; but no nation not secure in its dominion of the seas could have undertaken such a war as England then had to wage, and it was perhaps only the paramount sea power of this country that prevented the conflict taking a form and assuming dimensions that would have taxed British endurance to the uttermost and must almost certainly have entailed the loss of South Africa to the Empire. Certain naval features of the Cuban War between Spain and the United States, and of the War in the Far East between Russia and Japan, will be more conveniently considered in subsequent chapters of this manual.

The normal correlation and interdependence of naval and military forces in the armed conflict of national wills is sufficiently illustrated by the foregoing examples. In certain abnormal and exceptional cases each can act and produce the desired effect without the other. In a few extreme cases it is hard to see how either could act at all. If, for instance, Spain and Switzerland were to fall out, how could either attack the other ? They have no common frontier, and though Spain has a navy, Switzerland has no seaboard. Cases where naval conflict alone has decided the issue are those of the early wars between England and Holland. Neither could reach the other except across the sea, there was no territorial issue directly involved, and the object of both combatants was to secure a monopoly of maritime commerce. But as territorial issues, and territorial issues involving the sea and affected by it directly or indirectly, are nearly always at stake in great wars, history affords few examples of great international conflicts in which sea power does not enter as a factor, often of supreme importance.

It must of course enter as a factor of paramount importance in any war between an insular State and a continental one—as in the war between Russia and Japan—or between two continental States which—as in the war between Spain and the United States—have no common frontier on land. War being the armed conflict of national wills, it is manifest that the opposing wills cannot in cases such as these be brought into armed conflict unless one State or the other is in a position to operate on the sea. The first move in such a conflict must of necessity be made, by one belligerent or the other, on the sea. This involves the conception of "the command of the sea," and as this is the fundamental conception of naval warfare as such, our analysis of naval warfare must begin with an exposition of what is meant by the command of the sea.

CHAPTER II

WE have seen that when two States go to war the primary object of each is to subdue and if possible to destroy the armed forces of the other. Until that is done either completely, or to such an extent as to induce the defeated belligerent to submit, the conflict of wills cannot be determined, and the two States cannot return to those normal relations, involving no violence or force, which constitute a state of peace. If they have a common frontier this circumstance indicates what is, as a general rule, the best and most efficient way of securing the object to be attained. The armed forces of both belligerents lie at the outset within their respective frontiers. If those of either can be constrained by the superior strategy of the other to keep within their own territory, the initial advantage lies with the belligerent who has so constrained them, and the war has in common parlance been carried into the enemy's country. In other words, the invasion of the enemy's territory has begun, and pressure has been brought to bear on his will which, if maintained without intermission and with an intensity duly

11

proportioned to its growing extent, must in the end subdue it. To this there is no alternative. To invade the enemy's territory at all is to inflict a reverse on his armed forces, which would assuredly have prevented the invasion if they could. The territory in the rear of the invading army is in greater or less degree brought under the control of the invader and thereby temporarily lost to the invaded State. If this process is continued the authority and the resources of the invaded State are progressively diminished, until at last when the capital is occupied and the remainder of the invaded country lies open to the advance of the invader, the defeated State must sue for peace on such terms as the invader may concede, because it has nothing left to fight for, and no force wherewithal to fight. This is of course merely an abstract and generalized description of the course of a war on land, but I need not consider its concrete details nor analyse any of the conditions which may, and in the concrete often do, impede or deflect its course, because my sole purpose is to show how armed force operates in the abstract to subdue the will of the belligerent who is worsted in the conflict. It operates by the destruction of his armed forces, by the occupation of his territory, and by the consequent extinction of his authority and appropriation of his resources. He can only recover the latter and liberate his territory by submitting

to such terms as the invader may dictate or
concede.

Naval warfare aims at the same primary object,
namely, the destruction of the enemy's armed forces
afloat ; but it cannot by itself produce the same
decisive effect, because there is no territory which
naval force, as such, can occupy and appropriate.
The sea is not territory. It is not nor can it be
made subject to the authority of an enemy in the
same sense that the land can, nor does it possess any
resources in itself such as on the land can be appropriated to the disadvantage and ultimate discomfiture
of a belligerent whose territory has been invaded.
The sea is the common highway of all nations, and
the exclusive possession of none. Apart from its
fisheries, which, outside the territorial waters of
any particular State, are open to all nations, it is
of no use, except as a highway, to any State. But
its use as a highway is the root of all sea power,
the foundation of all naval warfare. It is only
by this highway that an island State can be invaded, only by this highway that an island State,
or a State having no common frontier with its
adversary, can encounter and subdue the armed
forces of the enemy, whether on sea or on land.

Moreover, the sea as a highway differs in many
important respects from such highways or other
lines of communication as serve for the transit

and transport of armed forces and their necessary
supplies on land. In one sense it is all highway,
that is, it can be traversed in every direction by ships,
wherever there is water enough for them to float.
For military purposes land transit is confined to
such highways as are suitable to the march of an
army accompanied by artillery and heavy baggage
and supply trains, or to such railways as can more
expeditiously serve the same purpose. Hence an
army advancing in an enemy's country cannot advance on a very broad front, nor can it outmarch
its baggage and other supplies except for a very
limited time and for some exceptional purpose. Sea
transport is subject to no such limitations. Ships
carry their own supplies with them, and a fleet of
ships, whether of transports or of warships, can move
on as broad a front as is compatible with the exercise of due control over their combined movements.
Moreover, within certain limits and with certain
exceptions, where the waters to be traversed are
narrow, ships and fleets can vary their line of transit and advance to such an extent as to render the
discovery of their whereabouts a matter of some
difficulty. The same conditions affect the transit
of such merchant vessels as, carrying the flag of
one belligerent, are liable to capture by the other.
Hence the primary aim of all naval warfare is and
must be so to control the lines of communication

which traverse the seas affected, that the enemy cannot move his warships from one point to another without encountering a superior force of his adversary, and that his merchant ships cannot prosecute their voyages without running extreme risk of capture by the way. This is called, in time-honoured phraseology, securing the command of the sea, and the true meaning of this phrase is nothing more nor less than the effective control of all such maritime communications as are or can be affected by the operations of either belligerent. This control may extend, according to circumstances, to all the navigable seas of the globe, or it may be confined, for all practical purposes, to the waters adjacent to the respective territories of the two belligerents. In theory, however, its effect is unlimited, and so it must be in practice, where the territories of one belligerent or the other are widely scattered over the globe. That is the sense in which " the sea is all one."

It is important to note that the phrase " command of the sea " has no definite meaning except in war. In time of peace no State claims to command the sea or to control it in any way. But in any war in which naval force is engaged each belligerent seeks to secure the command of the sea for himself and to deny it to his enemy, that is to close the highway which the sea affords in time of peace to his war-ships and his merchant vessels alike. As regards the enemy's warships, moreover, he seeks to secure his own command by their destruction or capture. This is not always possible, because if the naval forces of the two belligerents are very unequally matched, it is always open to the weaker of the two to decline the conflict by keeping his main fleets in ports unassailable by naval force alone, and seeking to reduce the superiority of his adversary by assailing him incessantly with torpedo craft. He may also attempt the hazardous enterprise of sending out isolated cruisers to prey upon his adversary's commerce afloat. But in the case supposed, where the superiority of one side is so great as to compel the main fleets of the other to seek the protection of their fortified ports, such an enterprise is, as I shall show in a subsequent chapter, not only extremely hazardous in itself, but quite incapable of inflicting such loss on the superior adversary as would be likely to induce him to abandon the conflict.

Nevertheless the command of the sea is not established, or at best it is only partially, and it may be only temporarily, established by driving the main fleets of the enemy into ports which are inaccessible to naval force alone. They must not only be driven there but compelled to remain there. This has generally been done in the past, and according to many, but not all, naval authorities, it will generally have to be done in the future by the operation known as blockade, whereby the enemy is prevented from coming out, or is compelled if he does come out to fight a superior force lying in wait outside. As a matter of fact, inasmuch as a blockade to be really deterrent must be conducted by a blockading force superior to that which is blockaded—for otherwise the latter need not shun an engagement in the open with the former—it can rarely be the interest of the blockader to prevent the exit of his adversary, since by the hypothesis if he could get him out he could beat him. But the blockade must nevertheless be maintained, because, although the blockaded fleet cannot by that means be destroyed, it can, at any rate, be immobilized and wiped off the board so long as it remains where it is.

The situation in which a blockade is set up by one belligerent and submitted to by the other is not identical with an effective command of the sea, though in certain circumstances it may approximate very closely to it. The blockaded forces may not be so thoroughly intimidated by the superior forces of the blockaders that they could not or would not, if they could, seek a favourable opportunity for breaking or evading the blockade imposed upon them. They may merely be waiting in a position unassailable by naval force alone until the blockading forces are so weakened through incessant torpedo attack, through the wear and tear inflicted on them

B

by the nature of the service on which they are engaged, through stress of weather, through the periodical necessity which compels even the best found ships to withdraw temporarily from the blockade for the purposes of repair, refit, and replenishment of their stores, and through the fatigue imposed on their officers and crews by the incessant vigilance which a blockade requires as to afford them a favourable opportunity of challenging a decision in the open. Or, again, if the forces of the blockaded belligerent are distributed between two or more of his fortified ports, he may attempt an evasion of the blockade at two or more of them for the purpose of combining the forces thus liberated and attacking one or more of the blockading fleets in superior force before they can re-establish their own superiority by concentration. Broadly speaking, this was the plan of operations adopted, or rather attempted, by Napoleon in the memorable campaign which ended at Trafalgar. It was frustrated by the persistent energy of Nelson, by the masterly dispositions of Barham at the Admiralty, by the tenacity with which Cornwallis maintained the blockade at Brest, and by the instinctive sagacity with which other commanders of the several blockading and cruising squadrons nearly always did the right thing at the right moment, divined Barham's purpose, and carried it out almost automatically. Practically, Napoleon was beaten and his projected invasion of England was abandoned many weeks before Trafalgar was won. But the command of the sea was not thereby secured to England. It needed Trafalgar and the destruction of the French and Spanish Fleets there accomplished to effect that consummation. England thenceforth remained in effective and almost un-disputed command of the sea, and the Peninsular campaigns of Wellington were for the first time rendered possible. The contrasted phases of the conflict before and after Trafalgar are perhaps the best illustration in history of the vast and vital difference between a command of the sea in dispute and a command of the sea established. Trafalgar was the turning-point in the long conflict between England and Napoleon.

CHAPTER III

I HAVE so far treated blockade as the initial stage of a struggle for the command of the sea. That appears to me to be the logical order of treatment, because when two naval Powers go to war it is almost certain that the stronger of the two will at the outset attempt to blockade the naval forces of the other. The same thing is likely to happen even if the two are approximately equal in naval force, but in that case the blockade is not likely to be of long duration, because both sides will be eager to obtain a decision in the open. The command of the sea is a matter of such vital moment to both sides that each must needs seek to obtain it as soon and as completely as possible, and the only certain way to obtain it is by the destruction of the armed forces of the enemy. The advantage of putting to sea first is in naval warfare the equivalent or counterpart of the advantage in land warfare of first crossing the enemy's frontier. If that advantage is pushed home and the enemy is still unready it must lead to a blockade. It is, moreover, quite possible that even if both belligerents are equally ready—I am here assuming them to be approximately equal in force—one or other, if not both, may think it better strategy to await developments before risking everything in an attempt to secure an immediate decision. In point of fact, the difference between this policy and the policy of a declared blockade is, as I am about to show, almost imperceptible, especially in modern conditions of naval warfare. It is therefore necessary to consider the subject of blockade more in detail. Other subjects closely associated with this will also have to be considered in some detail before we can grasp the full purport and extent of what is meant by the command of the sea.

There are two kinds of blockade—military and commercial. The former includes the latter, but the latter does not necessarily involve the former, except in the sense that armed naval force is necessary to maintain it. By a commercial blockade a belligerent seeks to intercept the maritime commerce of the enemy, to prevent any vessels, whether enemy or neutral, from reaching his ports, and at the same time to prevent their egress to the same extent. This in certain circumstances may be a very effective agency for bending or breaking the enemy's will and compelling his submission, but I reserve its consideration for more detailed treatment hereafter. It is with military blockade that I am here more especially concerned.

We have seen that the paramount purpose of all naval warfare, and, indeed, of all warfare, is the destruction of the armed forces of the enemy. His armed forces are in the last resort the sole instrument of his will, and their destruction to such an extent as is necessary to subdue his will is the sole agency by which peace can be restored. Whatever the extent of the war, whether it is limited or unlimited, in the sense assigned to those words by Clausewitz and his followers, the conflict of national wills out of which the quarrel arose must in some wáy be composed, either by concessions on both sides or by the complete subjection of one side to the other, before it can come to an end. It follows that the main object of a military blockade can rarely be to keep the enemy's forces sealed up, masked, and to that extent immobilized in the blockaded ports. Its real object is to secure that if they do come out they shall be observed, shadowed, and followed until such time as they can be encountered by a superior force, and if possible destroyed. The classical text on this topic is a letter written on August 1, 1804, by Nelson to the Lord Mayor of London, acknowledging a vote of thanks passed by the Corporation, and addressed to Nelson as commanding the fleet blockading Toulon. Nelson said in his reply : " I beg to inform your Lordship that the port of Toulon has never been blockaded by me : quite

the reverse—every opportunity has been offered to
the enemy to put to sea, for it is there that we hope
to realize the hopes and expectations of our country,
and I trust that they will not be disappointed."
What Nelson here meant was that the so-called
blockade of the port—it was a common, but, as
he held, an erroneous expression—was merely in-
cidental to the operation he was conducting.   His
main objective was the armed forces of the enemy
lying unassailable within the blockaded port.   He
could not make them put to sea but he gave them
every opportunity of doing so.   So far from wishing
to keep them in, his one desire was to get them out
into the open, " for it is there that we hope to realize
the hopes and expectations of our country "—
that is to get a decision in favour of the British
arms.

Now, this being the object of a military blockade,
its methods will be subordinated to that object.
In the days of sailing ships the method which com-
mended itself to the best naval authorities of the
time was to have an inshore squadron, consisting
mainly of frigates and smaller craft, but strengthened
if necessary by a few capital ships, generally two-
deckers, closely watching the entrance to the port,
but keeping outside the range of its land defences.
This was supported at a greater distance in the
offing by the main blockading fleet of heavier ships

of the line, cruising within narrow limits and keeping close touch with the inshore squadron. Such a method is no longer practicable owing to the development of steam navigation, and to the introduction into naval warfare of the locomotive torpedo, and of special vessels designed to make the attack of this weapon extremely formidable and extremely difficult to parry. The inshore squadron of the old days was liable to no attack which it could not parry if in sufficient force, and if too hardly pressed it could always fall back on the main blockading fleet, which was unassailable except by a corresponding force of the enemy. The advent of the torpedo and of its characteristic craft has changed all this. No naval Power can now afford to place its battleships at a fixed station, or even in close touch with a fixed rendezvous, which is within reach of an enemy's torpedo craft. The torpedo vessel which operates only on the surface is, it is true, formidable only at night; in the daytime it is powerless in attack and extremely vulnerable. But the submarine is equally formidable in the daytime, and its attack even in the daytime is far more insidious and difficult to parry than that of the surface torpedo vessel is at night. The effective range of the surface torpedo vessel is thus, for practical purposes, half the distance which it can traverse in any given direction from its base between dusk and dawn—say from one hundred to two hundred miles, according to its speed and the season of the year. The speed of the submarine is much less, but it can keep the sea for many days together, sinking beneath the surface whenever it is threatened with attack. It can also approach a battleship or fleet of battleships in the same submerged condition, and experience has already demonstrated that its advance in that condition to within striking distance is extremely difficult to detect. Moreover, even if its presence is detected in time, the only certain defence against it is for the battleship to steam away from it at a speed greater than any submarine has ever attained or is likely to attain in the submerged condition. It should further be noted that torpedo craft engaged in offensive operations of this character are not confined to the blockaded port as a base. Any sheltered anchorage will serve their purpose, provided it is sufficiently fortified to resist such attacks from the sea as may be anticipated.

Thus, in the conditions established by the advent of the torpedo and its characteristic craft, there would seem to be only two alternatives open to a fleet of battleships engaged in blockade operations. Either it must be stationed in some sheltered anchorage outside the radius of action of the enemy's surface torpedo craft, and if within that radius adequately defended against torpedo attack—as Togo established a flying base for the use of his fleet, first at the Elliot Islands and afterwards at Dalny, for the purpose of blockading Port Arthur ; or it must cruise in the open outside the same limits, keeping in touch with its advanced cruisers and flotillas by means of wireless telegraphy, and thereby dispensing with anything like a fixed rendezvous. It is not, perhaps, imperative that it should always cruise entirely outside the prescribed radius, because experience in modern naval manœuvres has frequently shown that it is a very difficult thing for torpedo craft, moving at random, to discover a fleet which is constantly shifting its position at high speed, especially when they are at any moment liable to attack from cruisers and torpedo craft of the other side.

Thus a modern blockade will, so far as battle fleets are concerned, be of necessity rather a watching blockade than a masking or sealing up blockade. If the two belligerents are unequal in naval strength it will probably take some such form as the following. The weaker belligerent will at the outset keep his battle fleet in his fortified ports. The stronger may do the same, but he will be under no such paramount inducement to do so. Both sides will, however, send out their torpedo craft and supporting cruisers with intent to do as much harm as they can to the armed forces of the enemy. If one belligerent can get his torpedo craft to sea before the enemy is ready, he will, if he is the stronger of the two, forthwith attempt to establish as close and sustained a watch of the ports sheltering the enemy's armed forces as may be practicable ; if he is the weaker, he will attempt sporadic attacks on the ports of his adversary and on such of his warships as may be found in the open. If the enemy is so incautious as to have placed any of his capital ships or other important craft in a position open to the assault of torpedo craft—as Russia did at Port Arthur at the opening of the war with Japan—or if he has been so lacking in vigilance and forethought as not to have taken timely and adequate measures for meeting sporadic attacks of the kind indicated, such attacks may be very effective and may even go so far to redress the balance of naval strength as to encourage the originally weaker belligerent to seek a decision in the open. But the forces of the stronger belligerent must be very badly handled and disposed for anything of the kind to take place. The advantage of superior force is a tremendous one. If it is associated with energy, determination, initiative, and skill of disposition no more than equal to those of the assailant, it is overwhelming. The sea-keeping capacity, or what has been called the enduring mobility, of torpedo craft, is comparatively small. Their coal-supply is limited, especially when they are steaming at full speed, and they carry no very large reserve of torpedoes. They must, therefore, very frequently return to a base to replenish their supplies. The superior enemy is, it is true, subject to the same disabilities, but being superior he has more torpedo craft to spare and more cruisers to attack the torpedo craft of the enemy and their own escort of cruisers. When the raiding torpedo craft return to their base he will make it very difficult for them to get in and just as difficult for them to get out again. He will suffer losses, of course, for there is no superiority of force that will confer immunity in that respect in war. But even between equal forces, equally well led and handled, there is no reason to suppose that the losses of one side will be more than equal to those of the other ; whereas if one side is appreciably superior to the other it is reasonable to suppose that it will inflict greater losses on the enemy than it suffers itself, while even if the losses are equal the residue of the stronger force will still be greater than that of the weaker. It is true that the whole art of war, whether on sea or on land, consists in so disposing your armed forces, both strategically and tactically, that you may be superior to the enemy at the critical point and moment, and that success in this supreme art is no inherent prerogative of the belligerent whose aggregate forces are superior to those of his adversary. But this is only to say that success in war is not an affair of numbers alone. It is an affair of numbers combined with hard fighting and skilful disposition.

CHAPTER IV

WE have seen that blockade is only a means to an end, that end being the destruction or surrender of the armed forces of the enemy. We have seen also that that end cannot be obtained by blockade alone. All that a military blockade can do is by a judicious disposition of superior force, either to prevent the enemy coming out at all, or to secure that if he does come out he shall be brought to action. The former method is only applicable where the blockader's superiority of force is so great that his adversary cannot venture at the outset to encounter his main fleets in the open, and in that case the establishment of a blockade of this character is for many purposes practically tantamount to securing the command of the sea to the blockader so long as the blockade can be maintained. Such a situation, however, can very rarely arise. There are very few instances of it in naval history, and there are likely to be fewer in the future than there have been in the past. The closest blockade ever established and maintained was that of Brest by Cornwallis from 1803 to 1805, when Napoleon was projecting the invasion

of England. Yet it would be too much to say that
during those strenuous years Ganteaume never could
have got out, had he been so minded, and it is not
to be forgotten that for some time during the crisis
of the campaign he was forbidden by Napoleon
to make the attempt. Moreover, such a situation,
even when it does arise, amounts at best to a stale-
mate, not to a checkmate. It leaves the enemy's
fleet " a fleet in being," immobilized and wiped off
the board for the moment, but nevertheless so
operating as to immobilize the blockading fleet in
so far as the chief effort of the latter must be concentrated on maintaining the blockade.

It is necessary to dwell at some length on this
conception of " a fleet in being." Admiral Mahan,
the great historian of sea power—whose high
authority all students of naval warfare will readily
acknowledge and rarely attempt to dispute—speaks
of it in his *Life of Nelson* as a doctrine or opinion
which " has received extreme expression . . . and
apparently undergone extreme misconception."
On the other hand, Admiral Sir Cyprian Bridge tells
us in the *Encyclopædia Britannica* (*s.v.* " Sea-
Power ") that " the principle of the ' fleet in being '
lies at the bottom of all sound strategy." Of a
principle which, according to one high authority,
lies at the bottom of all sound strategy, and according
to another has received extreme expression and

undergone misconception equally extreme, it is plainly essential that a true conception should be obtained before it can be applied to the elucidation of any of the problems of naval warfare. Now what is this much-debated principle ? It is best to go to the fountain-head for its elucidation. The phrase " a fleet in being " was first used by Arthur Herbert, Earl of Torrington, in his defence before the Court Martial which tried and acquitted him for his conduct of the naval campaign of 1690, and especially of the Battle of Beachy Head, which was the leading event—none too glorious for British arms—of that campaign. " Both as a strategist and as a tactician," says Admiral Bridge, " Torrington was immeasurably ahead of his contemporaries. The only English admirals who can be placed above him are Hawke and Nelson." Yet he was regarded by many of his contemporaries, and has been represented by many historians, merely as the incapable seaman who failed to win the Battle of Beachy Head, and thereby jeopardized the safety of the kingdom at a very critical time.

The situation was as follows. The country was divided between the partisans of James II. and the supporters of William III. James was in Ireland, where his strength was greatest, and William had gone thither to encounter him, his transit having been covered by a small squadron of six men-of-war,

under the command of Sir Cloudesley Shovel. The
army was with William in Ireland, and Great Britain
could only be defended on land by a hastily levied
militia. Its sole effective defence was the fleet ;
and the fleet, although reinforced by a Dutch contingent, was, for the moment, insufficient to defend
it. The chief reliance of James was upon the friendship and forces, naval and military, of Louis XIV.
Here was a case in which the security of England
against insurrection at home and invasion from
abroad depended on the sufficiency and capacity
of her fleets to maintain the command of the sea—
that is, either to defeat the enemy's naval forces
or to keep them at bay, and thereby to deny freedom
of transit to any military forces that Louis might
attempt to launch against British territory. The
French king resolved to make a determined attempt
to wrest the command of the sea from his adversaries,
and by overpowering the allied fleets of England
and Holland in the Channel, to open the way for a
successful invasion and a successful insurrection
to follow. A great fleet was collected at Brest,
under the supreme command of Tourville, and a
squadron from Toulon under Château-Renault was
ordered to join him in the Channel, so as to enable
him to threaten London, to foment a Jacobite
insurrection in the capital, to land troops in
Torbay, and to occupy the Irish Channel in such

c

force as to prevent the return of William and his army.

Now, of course, none of these objects could be attained unless the allied fleets in the Channel and adjacent waters could be either decisively defeated in the open or else so intimidated by the superior forces of the enemy as to decline a conflict and retire to some place of safety. On the broad principle that the paramount object of all warfare is the destruction of the armed forces of the enemy, Tourville, if he felt himself strong enough, was bound to seek out the allied fleet and challenge it to a decisive combat. On the same principle, Torrington, if he felt himself strong enough, was bound to pursue the same aggressive strategy, and by thoroughly beating the French to frustrate all their objects at once. But Torrington was not strong enough and knew that he was not strong enough. He had foreseen the crisis and warned his superiors betimes, entreating them to take adequate measures for dealing with it. They took no such measures. On the contrary, the dispositions they made were calculated rather to aggravate the danger than to avert it. Early in the year a fleet of sixteen sail of the line under Killigrew had been sent in charge of a convoy to Cadiz with orders to prevent, if possible, the exit of the Toulon fleet from the Mediterranean and to follow it up should it make good its escape. This strategy was unimpeachable if only Killigrew could make sure of intercepting Château-Renault and defeating him, and if the naval forces left in home waters when Killigrew was detached were sufficient to give a good account of the fleet that Tourville was collecting at Brest. But in its results it was disastrous, for Killigrew, delayed by weather and by the many preoccupations, commercial and strategic, entailed by his instructions was unable either to bar the passage of the Toulon fleet or to overtake it during its progress towards the Channel. Hence Château-Renault was able to effect his junction with Tourville unmolested, while Killigrew did not reach Plymouth until after the battle of Beachy Head had been fought, when, Tourville being victorious in the Channel, he was obliged to carry his squadron into the Hamoaze so as to be out of harm's way. Shovel, having escorted the king and his troops to Ireland, was equally unable to carry out his orders to join Torrington in the Channel, since Tourville stood in the way. Hence, although fully alive to the strategic value, in certain contingencies, of the forces under Killigrew and Shovel, Torrington was compelled to rely mainly on the force under his immediate command, the insufficiency of which he had many months before pointed out and vainly implored his superiors to redress.

The result of all this was that no adequate steps

were, or could be, taken, to prevent the advance of
Tourville in greatly superior force into the Channel.
Torrington hoisted his flag in the Downs at the end
of May, and even then the Dutch contingent had not
joined in the numbers promised. Hence it was
impossible to keep scouts out to the westward as
the Dutch had undertaken to do, and the first
definite intelligence that Torrington received of
the advance of the French was the information
that on June 23 they were anchored in great force
to the westward of the Isle of Wight. Three days
later, having in the meanwhile received a Dutch
reinforcement bringing his force up to fifty-five
sail of the line and twenty fire-ships, he offered
them battle in that position, but it was declined.
His own comment on this hazardous adventure
may here be quoted : " I do acknowledge my first
intention of attacking them, a rashness that will
admit of no better excuse than that, though I did
believe them stronger than we are, I did not believe
it to so great a degree. . . . Their great strength
and caution have put soberer thoughts into my head,
and have made me very heartily give God thanks
they declined the battle yesterday ; and indeed I
shall not think myself very unhappy if I can get rid
of them without fighting, unless it may be upon
equaller terms than I can at present see any prospect
of. . . . A council of war I called this morning

unanimously agreed we are by all manner of means
to shun fighting with them, especially if they have
the wind of us ; and retire, if we cannot avoid it
otherwise, even to the Gunfleet, the only place we
can with any manner of probability make our account
good with them in the condition we are in. We have
now had a pretty good view of their fleet, which
consists of near, if not quite, eighty men-of-war fit
to lie in a line and thirty fire-ships ; a strength that
puts me beside hopes of success, if we should fight,
and really may not only endanger the losing of the
fleet, but at least the quiet of our country too ;
for if we are beaten they, being absolute masters
of the sea, will be at great liberty of doing many
things they dare not attempt while we observe them
and are in a possibility of joining Vice-Admiral
Killigrew and our ships to the westward. If I find
a possibility, I will get by them to the westward
to join those ships ; if not, I mean to follow the result
of the council of war."

The strategy here indicated is plain, and, in my
judgment, sound. It may be profitably compared
with that of Nelson as explained to his captains
during his return from the West Indies whither he
had pursued Villeneuve. Villeneuve was on his
way back to European waters and Nelson hoped to
overtake him. He had eleven ships of the line in
his fleet and Villeneuve was known to have not less

than eighteen. Yet, though Nelson did not shrink from an engagement on his own terms, he was resolved not to force one inopportunely. " Do not," he said to his captains, " imagine I am one of those hot-brained people who fight at immense disadvantage without an adequate object. My object is partly gained "—that is, Villeneuve had been driven out of the West Indies. " If we meet them we shall find them not less than eighteen, I rather think twenty, sail of the line, and therefore do not be surprised if I do not fall on them immediately ; we won't part without a battle. I think they will be glad to leave me alone, if I will let them alone ; which I will do, either till we approach the shores of Europe, or they give an advantage too tempting to be resisted." Torrington's attitude was the same as Nelson's, except perhaps that he lacked the ardent faith to say with Nelson, " We won't part without a battle." He would not think himself very unhappy if he could get rid of Tourville without a battle. But the situations of the two men were different. Nelson knew, as he said himself, that " by the time that the enemy has beat our fleet soundly, they will do us no harm this year." If, that is, by the sacrifice of eleven ships of his own he could wipe out eighteen or twenty of the enemy, destroying some and disabling as many as he could of the rest, he would leave the balance of naval force still strongly in favour of his country, more strongly in fact than if he fought no action at all. Torrington, on the other hand, knew that " if we are beaten they, being absolute masters of the sea, will be at great liberty of doing many things they dare not attempt while we observe them and are in a possibility of joining Vice-Admiral Killigrew and our ships to the westward." Killigrew and Shovel had twenty-two sail of the line between them, and Torrington, in the dispatch above quoted, had requested that they should be ordered to advance to Portsmouth, whence, if the French pursued him to the eastward, they might be able to join him " over the flats " of the Thames. As he had fifty-five sail of the line himself, with a possibility of reinforcements from Chatham, the concentration off the Thames of the whole of the forces available would have enabled him to encounter Tourville on something like equal terms ; and from that, assuredly, he would not have shrunk. Meanwhile he would wait, watch, observe, and pursue a defensive strategy. If Tourville should withdraw to the westward he would follow him and get past him if he could, and in that case, having picked up Killigrew and Shovel, he would be in a position to take the offensive on no very unequal terms and not to part from Tourville without a battle.

But the strategy of Torrington—admirable and unimpeachable as, according to such high authorities

as Admiral Bridge and the late Admiral Colomb,
it was—did not at all commend itself to Mary and
her Council, who, during William's absence in
Ireland, were left in charge of the kingdom. They
wanted a battle, although Torrington had plainly
told them that it could not be a victory and might
result in a disastrous and even fatal defeat. " We
apprehend," they said in a dispatch purporting
to come from Mary herself, " the consequences of
your retiring to the Gunfleet to be so fatal, that we
choose rather you should, upon any advantage of
the wind, give battle to the enemy than retreat
further than is necessary to get an advantage upon
the enemy." Torrington, of course, never intended
to retire to the Gunfleet—which was an anchorage
protected by sandbanks off the coast of Essex to
the north of the Thames—if he could avoid doing so.
But unless he went there, there was no advantage
to be got upon the enemy by retreating to the
eastward, because there alone could he get reinforcements from Chatham and possibly be joined by
Killigrew and Shovel " over the flats "; which
is what he meant by saying that the Gunfleet was
" the only place we can with any manner of probability make our account with them in the position
we are in." On the other hand, if the French gave
him an opportunity he would, if he could, get past
them to the westward and there join Killigrew and

Shovel in a position of much greater advantage. But in his actual situation, not being one of " those hot-brained people who fight at immense disadvantage without an adequate object," he knew that a battle was the last thing which he ought to risk and the first that the French must desire. However, as a loyal seaman, who knew how to obey orders, he did as he was told. The French had pressed him as far as Beachy Head and there he gave battle, taking care so to fight as to risk as little as possible. He was beaten, as he expected to be, and the Dutch, who had been the most hotly engaged, were very severely handled by the French. But though his losses were considerable, for he had to destroy some of his ships to prevent their falling into the hands of the enemy, he saved his fleet from the destruction which must have befallen it had he fought otherwise than he did. As the day advanced and the battle raged, the wind dropped and the tide began to ebb. Torrington, taking advantage of this, anchored his fleet, while the French drifted away to the west-ward. When the tide again began to flow he again took advantage of it and retreated to the eastward. The French made some show of pursuit, but Torring-ton made good his retreat into the Thames, where, the buoys having been taken up, the French could not follow him. Finally, the French withdrew from the Channel, having accomplished nothing beyond an insignificant raid on Teignmouth. Torrington was tried by Court Martial and acquitted, though he was never again employed afloat. But the fact remains that, as Admiral Bridge says, " most seamen were at the time, have been since, and still are in agreement with Torrington." As to his conduct of the battle, which has so unjustly involved him in lasting discredit with the historians, though not with the seamen, he said in his defence before the Court Martial : " I may be bold to say that I have had time and cause enough to think of it, and that, upon my word, were the battle to be fought over again, I do not know how to mend it, under the same circumstances." Again, as to his general conduct of the campaign, he said : " It is true that the French made no great advantage of their victory though they put us to a great charge in keeping up the militia ; but had I fought otherwise, our fleet had been totally lost, and the whole kingdom had lain open to an invasion. What, then, would have become of us in the absence of his Majesty and most of the land forces ? As it was, most men were in fear that the French would invade ; but I was always of another opinion ; for I always said that, *whilst we had a fleet in being*, they would not dare to make an attempt."

This is the first appearance of the phrase " a fleet in being " in the terminology of naval warfare.

Its reappearance in our own day and its frequent employment in naval discussion are due to the masterly analysis of Torrington's strategy and tactics which the late Admiral Colomb gave in his illuminating work on *Naval Warfare*. In order to avoid giving it the extreme expression which, according to Admiral Mahan, it has received from some writers, and involving it in that extreme misconception which he thinks it has undergone at the hands of others—or it may be of the same—I have thought it worth while to examine at some length the campaign which gave rise to it so as to ascertain exactly what was in the mind of Torrington when he first used it. It is plain that Torrington held, as all great seamen have held, that the primary object of every belligerent is to destroy the armed forces of the enemy. He was so circumstanced that he could not do that himself, because the forces which might have been at his disposal for the purpose, had the circumstances been other than they were, were so divided and dispersed that the enemy might overcome them in detail. That the enemy would do this, if he could, he did not doubt, and it was equally certain that it must be his immediate object to prevent his doing it. His own force being by far the strongest of the three opposed to Tourville, it must be upon him that the brunt of the conflict would fall. Nothing would suit him better than that Tourville

should turn back and attempt to force a battle
on either Killigrew or Shovel to the westward,
because in that case he could hang upon Tourville's
rear and flanks and take any opportunity that
offered to get past him and concentrate the British
forces to the westward of him. But Tourville
gave him no such opportunity. He pressed him hard
and might have pressed him back even to the
Gunfleet if Torrington had not been ordered by Mary
and her advisers to give battle " upon any advantage
of the wind." But even in fighting the battle, which
his own judgment told him ought not to be fought,
he never lost sight of the paramount necessity
of so fighting it as to give Tourville no decisive
advantage. The victory was a barren one to
Tourville. It gave him no command of the sea and
for that reason he was unable to prosecute any enterprise of invasion. The command of the sea remained in dispute, and unless the dispute could be
decided in Tourville's favour he would have fought
and won the battle of Beachy Head in vain, as the
event showed that he did. Torrington held that
his " fleet in being," even after the reverse at Beachy
Head, was a sufficient bar to the further enterprises
of Tourville, nor can Tourville's subsequent action
be explained on any other hypothesis than that he
shared Torrington's opinion and acted on it.

The truth is, that the doctrine of the fleet in

being, as understood and illustrated by Torrington, is in reality the counterpart and complement of the doctrine of the command of the sea as expounded above. " I consider," said the late Sir Geoffrey Hornby, a strategist and tactician of unrivalled authority in his time, " that I have command of the sea when I am able to tell my Government that they can move an expedition to any point without fear of interference from an enemy's fleet." This condition cannot be satisfied so long as the enemy has a fleet in being, that is a fleet strategically at large, not itself in command of the sea, but strong enough to deny that command to its adversary by strategic and tactical dispositions adapted to the circumstances of the case. Thus command of the sea and a fleet in being are mutually exclusive terms. So long as a hostile fleet is in being there is no command of the sea ; so soon as the command of the sea is established there is no hostile fleet in being. Each of these propositions is the complement of the other.

Nevertheless, the mere statement of these abstract propositions solves none of the concrete problems of naval warfare. War is not governed by phrases. It is governed by stern and inexorable realities. The question whether a particular fleet in any particular circumstances is or is not a fleet in being is not a question of theory, it is a question of fact. The answer to it depends on the spirit, purpose, tenacity, and strategic insight of those who control its movements. No fleet is a fleet in being unless inspired by what may be called the *animus pugnandi*, that is, unless, if and when the opportunity offers, it is prepared to strike a blow at all hazards. For this reason the Russian fleet in Sebastopol at the time of the invasion of the Crimea was not a fleet in being, although it had a splendid opportunity, which a Nelson would assuredly have found too tempting to be resisted, of showing its mettle when the French warships were employed as transports ; and the allies might have been made to pay heavily for their neglect to blockade it had it been inspired by an effective *animus pugnandi*. On the other hand, the four ill-fated Spanish cruisers which crossed the Atlantic to take part in the Cuban war were a true fleet in being, however inferior and forlorn, and were so regarded by the United States authorities so long as they remained strategically at large. Even when two of them and two destroyers were known to be in Santiago, the Secretary of the United States Navy telegraphed to Admiral Sampson, " Essential to know if all four Spanish cruisers in Santiago. Military expedition must wait this information." The same thing happened in the war between Russia and Japan. The first act of Japan in that war was by a torpedo attack on the Russian fleet at Port Arthur, so to depress the *animus pugnandi* of the latter as practically to deprive it for a time of the character of a fleet in being—a character which it only partially recovered afterwards under the brief influence of the heroic but ill-fated Makaroff. This being accomplished, the invasion of Manchuria ensued as a matter of course. The ascendency thus established by the Japanese fleet at the outset, though assailed more than once, was nevertheless maintained throughout the subsequent operations until the Russian fleet at Port Arthur, deprived of the little character it ever possessed as a true fleet in being, was reduced to the condition of what Admiral Mahan has aptly called a "fortress fleet," and was surrendered at the fall of the fortress. Many other illustrations of the principle of the fleet in being might be given. The history of naval warfare is full of them. But they need not be multiplied as they all point the same moral. That moral is, that a fleet in being to be of any use must be inspired by a determined and persistent *animus pugnandi*. It must not be a mere "fortress fleet." Torrington can never have imagined for a moment that the fleet which, in spite of the disastrous orders of Mary and her council, he had saved from destruction, would by its mere existence prevent a French invasion. He had kept it in being in order that he might use it offensively whenever occasion should arise, well knowing that so long as it maintained that disposition Tourville would be paralysed for offence. "Whilst we observe the French," he said, "they cannot make any attempt on ships or shore without running a great hazard." Such hazards may be run for an adequate object, and to determine rightly when they may be run and when they may not is perhaps the most searching test of a naval commander's capacity and insight. It is a psychological question rather than a strategic one. Such a commander must know whether his adversary's *animus pugnandi* is so keen and so unflinching as to invest his fleet, albeit inferior, with the true character of a fleet in being, or whether, on the other hand, it is so feeble as to turn it into a mere fortress fleet. But that is only to say that in war the man always counts for far more than the machine, that the best commander is a man "with whom," as Admiral Mahan says of Nelson, "moral effect is never in excess of the facts of the case, whose imagination produces to him no paralysing picture of remote contingencies." *Bene ausus vana contemnere*, as Livy says of Alexander's conquest of Darius, is the eternal secret of successful war.

CHAPTER V

THE condition of disputed command of the sea is the normal condition at the outbreak of any war in which operations at sea are involved between two belligerents of approximately equal strength, or indeed between any two belligerents, the weaker of whom is sufficiently inspired by the *animus pugnandi*—or it may be by other motives rather political than strategic in character—to try conclusions with his adversary in the open. This follows immediately from the nature of command of the sea, which is, it will be remembered, the effective control over the maritime communications of the waters in dispute. I must here repeat, that the phrase command of the sea has no definite meaning in time of peace. No nation nowadays seeks in time of peace to control maritime communications, that is, to exercise any authority or constraint over any ships, whether warships or merchant vessels—other than those flying its own flag—which traverse the seas on their lawful occasions. There was, indeed, a time when England claimed what was called the " sovereignty of the seas," that is, the right to exact at all times certain marks of deference to her flag, in the form of certain salutes of ceremony, from all ships traversing the seas surrounding the British Islands, the narrow seas as they were called. But that is an entirely different thing from the command of the sea in a strategic sense, and has in fact no connection with it. It has long been abandoned and it need only be mentioned here in order to be carefully distinguished from the latter. Any nation seeking to exercise or secure the command of the sea in this sense would in so doing engage in an act of war, and would be regarded as so engaging by any other nation whose rights and interests were in any way affected by the act. Hence the difference between the two is plain. The claim to the sovereignty of the seas and the exaction of the ceremonial observance—the lowering of a flag or a sail—which symbolized it, was not in itself an act of war, though it might lead to war if the claim were resisted. An attempt to assert or secure the command of the sea is, on the other hand, in itself an act of war and would never be made by any nation not prepared to take the consequence in the instant outbreak of hostilities.

For what is it that a nation seeks to do when it attempts to exercise or secure the command of the sea? It seeks to do nothing more and nothing less than to deny freedom of access to the waters in dispute to the ships, whether warships or merchant ships, of some other nation.   It denies the common right of highway, which is the essential attribute of the sea, to that other nation, and seeks to secure the monopoly of that right for itself. In other words, it seeks to drive its adversary's warships from the sea, and either by the capture of his merchant vessels to appropriate the wealth they contain or by destroying them to deprive the adversary of its enjoyment. This is all that naval warfare as such can do.   If the enemy is not constrained by the destruction of his warships and the extinction of his maritime commerce to submit to his victorious adversary's will, other agencies, not exclusively naval in character, must be employed to bring about that consummation. This means that military force must be brought into operation, either for the invasion of the defeated adversary's territory or for the occupation of some of his possessions lying across the seas, if he has any. If he has none, or if such as he has are not worth taking or holding—either as a permanent possession or as what is called a material guarantee to be used in the subsequent negotiations for peace—then the only alternative is invasion.   But that is a subject which demands a chapter to itself.

It rarely happens, however, that a great naval Power is devoid of transmarine possessions altogether, or that such as it holds are esteemed by it to be of

so little value or importance that their seizure by
an enemy would leave matters *in statu quo*. Sea
power is, as a rule, the outcome of a flourishing
maritime commerce. Maritime commerce as it
expands, tends, even apart from direct colonization,
to bring territorial occupation in its train. The
origin and history of the British rule in India is a
signal illustration of this tendency. There are other
causes of territorial expansion across the seas, as
Admiral Mahan has pointed out in his latest work
on *Naval Strategy*, but it is a rule which admits
of no exceptions that territorial possessions across
the seas, however they may have been acquired,
compel the Power which holds them to develop a
navy which, in the last resort, must be capable
of defending them. It was not, indeed, the needs of
maritime commerce which induced the United States
to acquire Puerto Rico and the Philippines. Their
acquisition was, as it were, a by-product of victorious sea power. But the vast expansion of the
United States Navy which the last dozen years have
witnessed is the direct result and the logical consequence of their acquisition.

Applying these principles to the defence of the
British Empire we see at once that the command
of the sea, in the sense already defined, is essential
to its successful prosecution. The case is not merely
exceptional, it is absolutely unique. The British

Isles might recover from the effects of a successful invasion, as other countries have done in like case. But the destruction of their maritime commerce would ruin them irretrievably, even if no invasion were undertaken. Half the maritime commerce of the world is carried on under the British flag. The whole of that commerce would be suppressed if an enemy once secured the command of the sea. The British Isles would be starved out in a few weeks. Whether an enemy so situated would decide to invade or invest—that is, so to impede our commerce that only an insignificant fraction of it could by evasion reach our ports—is a question not so much of strategy as of the economics of warfare. But really it hardly matters a pin which he decided to do. We should have to submit in either case. What would happen to our Dominions, Dependencies, and Colonies is plain. Those which are defenceless the enemy would seize if he thought it worth his while. In the case supposed they could obtain no military assistance from the mother-country. But those which could defend themselves he would have to overcome, if he could, by fighting. The great Dominions of the Empire would not fall into an enemy's lap merely because he had compelled the United Kingdom to sue for peace. To subdue them by force of arms would be a very formidable undertaking.

Such are the tremendous effects of an adverse

command of the sea on an insular kingdom and an
oceanic empire, which carries on—not by virtue of
any artificial monopoly, but solely by virtue of its
hardly won ascendency in the economic struggle
for existence—half the maritime commerce of the
world. On the other hand, its effects on any nation
which does not depend on the sea for its existence
can never be so overwhelming and may even be
insignificant. Germany was very little affected
by the command of the sea enjoyed by France
in the War of 1870. But in view of the enormous
growth of German maritime commerce in recent
years, a superiority of France at sea equal to
that which she enjoyed in 1870 would now be a
much more serious menace to Germany. In all
such cases the issue must be decided by military
operations suitable to the circumstances and the
occasion—operations in which naval force may take
an indispensable part even though it may not
directly decide the issue. It was, for example,
the United States army that captured Santiago and
secured the deliverance of Cuba ; but it was the
United States Navy alone that enabled the troops
to be in Cuba at all and to do what they did there.
Again, in the war between Russia and Japan it was
the capture of Port Arthur and the final overthrow
at Tsu-Shima of all that remained of Russia's
effective naval forces that induced Russia to entertain overtures for peace. But the reduction of

Port Arthur was mainly the work of the military arm and the continued successes of the Japanese armies in Manchuria must have contributed largely to Russia's surrender. These successes were, it is true, rendered possible by the Japanese Navy alone. It cannot be said that the Japanese ever held the undisputed command of the sea until after Tsu-Shima had been fought and won. But at the very outset of the war they established such an ascendency over the Russian naval forces in Far Eastern waters that the latter were in the end reduced to something less than even a "fortress fleet." At Port Arthur, writes Admiral Mahan, the fleet was "neither a fortress fleet, for except the guns mounted from it, the fleet contributed nothing to the defence of the place ; nor yet a fleet in being, for it was never used as such." Its *animus pugnandi* was fatally depressed on the first night of the war, and finally extinguished after the action of August 10.

The truth is, that in all the larger achievements of sea power—those, that is, to which a combination of naval and military force is indispensable—it is impossible to disengage the influence of one of these factors on the final issue from that of the other, and perhaps idle to attempt do to so. They act, as it were, like a chemical combination, not like the resultant of two separate but correlated mechanical forces, and their joint effect may be just as different from what might be the effect of either acting separately as water is different from the oxygen and hydrogen of which it is composed. But their operation in this wise can only begin after the command of the sea has been secured, or at least has been so far established as to reduce to a negligible quantity the risk of conducting military operations across seas of which the command is still nominally in dispute. Now there are several phases or stages in the enterprise of securing the command of the sea ; but they all depend on the power and the will to fight for it. There is no absolute command of the sea, except in the case of hostilities between two belligerents, separated by the sea, one of whom has no naval force at all. The solitary case in history of this situation is that of the War in South Africa. A similar situation would arise if one of two belligerents had completely destroyed all the effective naval force of the other. But that is a situation of which history affords few, if any, examples. Between these two extremes lies the whole history of naval warfare.

There is, moreover, one characteristic of naval warfare which has no exact counterpart in the conduct of military enterprises on land. This is the power which a naval belligerent has of withdrawing his sea-going force out of the reach of the sea-going force of the enemy by placing it in sheltered harbours too strongly fortified for the enemy to reduce by naval power alone. The only effective answer to this which the superior belligerent can make is, as has already been shown, to establish a blockade of the ports in question. This procedure is analogous to, but not identical with, the investment by military forces of a fortress in which an army has found shelter in the interior of the enemy's country. But the essential difference is that the land fortress can be completely invested so that no food or other supplies can reach it, whereas a sea fortress cannot, unless it is situated on a small island, be completely invested by naval force alone. In the one case, even if no assault is attempted, starvation must sooner or later bring about the surrender of the fortress together with any military force it contains, whereas in the other the blockaded port being, as a rule, in open communication with its own national territory, cannot be reduced by starvation. Moreover, for reasons already explained, a maritime fortress cannot nowadays be so closely blockaded as to prevent the exit of small craft almost at all times or even to prevent the exit of squadrons of battleships in circumstances favourable to the enterprise. Now the exit of small craft equipped for torpedo attack is a much more serious threat to the blockader than the exit of small craft, not so equipped, was in the old days of close blockade. In those days small craft could do no harm to ships of the line or even to frigates, whereas a torpedo craft is nowadays in certain circumstances the equal and more than the

equal of a battleship. For these reasons the escape
from a blockaded port of a squadron of battleships
might easily be regarded by the blockading enemy
as a less serious and even much more welcome
incident of the campaign than the frequent issue of
swarms of torpedo craft skilfully handled, daringly
navigated, and sternly resolved to do or die in the
attempt to reduce the battle superiority of the enemy.

It follows from these premisses that a naval
blockade—or a connected series of blockades—
can never be regarded as equivalent to an established
command of the sea. At its best it can only achieve
a temporary command of the sea in a state of unstable
and easily disturbed equilibrium. At its worst,
that is when it is least close and least effective,
and when the *animus pugnandi* of the enemy is
unimpaired and not to be intimidated, and is therefore ready at all times to take advantage of " an
opportunity too tempting to be resisted," it amounts
to a state of things in which the " fleet in being "
becomes the dominant factor of the situation.
It is mainly a psychological problem and scarcely
a strategic problem at all to determine when the
actual situation approximates to either of these
extremes, and the principle embodied in the words
bene ausus vana contemnere is the key to the solution
of this problem. If the blockaded fleet is merely
a fortress fleet, or not even that, as was the Russian
fleet at Port Arthur for some time after the first

night of the war, and even more after the critical
but indecisive conflict of August 10, then it is
legitimate, as Togo triumphantly showed, to regard
the situation so established as so far equivalent to
a temporary command of the sea that military
operations, involving the security of oversea transit
and the continuity of oversea supply, might be
undertaken with no greater risk than is always in-
separable from a vigorous initiative in war. But
had the Russian naval commanders been inspired—
as, perhaps, the ill-fated Makaroff alone was—with
a genuine *animus pugnandi*, they might have
perceived that their one chance of bringing all the
Japanese enterprises, naval and military, to nought,
was by fighting Togo's fleet " to a frazzle," even if
their own fleet perished in the conflict. Then the
Baltic Fleet, if it had any fight in it at all, must have
made short work of what remained of Togo's fleet,
and the Japanese communications with Manchuria
being thereby severed, Russia might have dictated
her own terms of peace. The real lesson of that war
is not that a true fleet in being can ever be safely
neglected, but that a fleet which can be neglected
with impunity is no true fleet in being. It should
never be forgotten that the problems of naval warfare are essentially psychological and not mechanical
in their nature. Their ultimate determining factors
are not material and ponderable forces operating
with measurable certainty, but those immaterial

and imponderable forces of the human mind and will which can be measured by no standard other than the result. By the material standard so popular in these days, and withal so full of fallacy, Nelson should have been defeated at Trafalgar and Rozhdestvensky should have been victorious at Tsu-Shima.

It is, of course, idle to press the doctrine of the command of the sea and the principle of the fleet in being so far as to affirm that no military enterprise of any kind can be prosecuted across the sea unless an unassailable command of the sea has first been established. Such a proposition is disallowed by the whole course of naval history, which is, in truth, for the most part, the history of the command of the sea remaining in dispute, often for long periods, between two belligerents, the balance inclining sometimes to one side and sometimes to the other, according to the fortune of war. The whole question is in the main one of degree and of circumstances. Broadly speaking, it may be said that the larger the military enterprise contemplated the more complete must be the command of the sea before it can be prosecuted with success and the more certain the assurance of its continuance in unimpaired efficiency until the objects of the enterprise are accomplished. Conversely, the strength, even if inferior, of the fleet in being, its strategic disposition, its tactical efficiency, and, above all, its *animus pugnandi* must all be accurately gauged by a naval commander before he can safely decide that a military expedition of any magnitude can be undertaken without fear of interference from an enemy's fleet. It was the neglect of these principles that ruined the Athenian expedition to Syracuse. It was equally the neglect of the same principles that entailed the failure of Napoleon's expedition to Egypt and the ultimate surrender of the army he had deserted there. It was the politic recognition of them that, as Admiral Mahan has shown in a brilliant passage, compelled Hannibal to undertake the arduous passage of the Alps for the purpose of invading Italy instead of transporting his troops by sea.

The limits of legitimate enterprise across seas of which the command although firmly gripped is not unassailably established, are perhaps best illustrated by the story of Craig's expedition to Malta and Sicily towards the close of the Trafalgar campaign. This remarkable episode, which has received less attention than it deserves from most historians, has been represented by Mr Julian Corbett in his instructive work on *The Campaign of Trafalgar* as the masterly offensive stroke by which Pitt hoped to abate, and, if it might be, to overthrow the military ascendency which Napoleon had established in

Europe. That view has not been universally accepted by Mr Corbett's critics, but the episode is entitled to close attention for the light it throws on the central problem of naval warfare. Pitt had concluded a treaty with Russia, which involved not merely naval but military co-operation with that Power in the Mediterranean. Craig's expedition was the shape which the military co-operation was to take. It consisted of some five thousand troops, and when it embarked in April 1805 it was convoyed by only two ships of the line in its transit over seas which, for all the Government which dispatched it knew, might be infested at the time by more than one fleet of the enemy.

Here, then, is a case in which the doctrine of the command of the sea and the principle of the fleet in being might seem to be violated in a crucial fashion. But the men who directed the arms of England in those days knew what they were about. Long before they allowed the expedition to start they had established a close and, as they thought, an effective blockade of all the Atlantic and Mediterranean ports in which either French or Spanish warships ready for sea were to be found. Nevertheless we have here a signal illustration of the essential difference between a command of the sea which has been made absolute by the destruction of the enemy's available naval forces—as was practically the case after Trafalgar—and one which is only virtual and potential, because, although the enemy's fleets have for the time been masked or sealed up in their ports, they may, should the fortune of war so determine, resume at any time the position and functions of a true fleet in being.   On the strength of a command of the sea of this merely contingent and potential character Pitt and his naval advisers had persuaded themselves that the way to the Mediterranean was open for the transit of troops.   Craig's transports, accordingly, put to sea on April 19.   But a week before Villeneuve with his fleet had left Toulon for the last time, had evaded Nelson's watch, and passing rapidly through the Straits, had called off Cadiz, and picking up such Spanish ships as were there had disappeared into space, no man knowing whither he had gone.   He might have gone to the East Indies, he might have gone to the West Indies, as in fact he did, or he might be cruising unmolested in waters where he could hardly fail to come across Craig's transports with their weak escort of two ships of the line.   It was a situation which no one had foreseen or regarded as more than a contingency too remote to be guarded against when Craig's expedition was allowed to start.   How Nelson viewed the situation may be seen from his reply to the Admiralty, written on his receipt of the first intimation that the expedition was about to start.

" As the ' Fisgard ' sailed from Gibraltar on the 9th
instant, two hours after the enemy's fleet from Toulon
had passed the Straits, I have to hope she would arrive
time enough in the Channel to give their Lordships
information of this circumstance *and to prevent
the Rear-Admiral and Troops before mentioned* "
—that is Craig's expedition—" *from leaving Spithead.*" In other words, Nelson held quite plainly
that had the Admiralty known that Villeneuve was
at sea outside the Straits they would not have
allowed Craig to start. That Nelson was right in
this assumption is proved by the fact that acting
on the inspiration of Barham—perhaps the greatest
strategist that ever presided at Whitehall—the Admiralty, as soon as they had grasped the situation,
sent orders to Calder off Ferrol, that if he came in
contact with the expedition he was to send it back to
Plymouth or Cork under cruiser escort and retain
the two ships of the line which had so far escorted
it under his own command. The fact was that if
Craig's expedition once passed Finisterre it would
find itself totally without the naval protection on
which the Admiralty relied when it was dispatched.
Villeneuve was outside the Straits no one knew where,
and had been reinforced by the Spanish ships from
Cadiz. Nelson, whose exact whereabouts was equally
unknown to the Admiralty, was detained in the
Mediterranean by baffling winds and also by the

necessity of making sure before quitting his station that Villeneuve had not gone to the Levant. Orde, who had been blockading Cadiz with a weak squadron which had to retire on Villeneuve's approach, had convinced himself, on grounds not without cogency, that Villeneuve was making for the northward, and had, quite correctly on this hypothesis, fallen back on the fleet blockading Brest, being ignorant of the peril to which Craig was exposed. Thus Craig's expedition seemed to be going straight to its doom unless Calder could intercept it and give it orders to return. However, Craig and Knight, whose flag flew in one of the ships of the line escorting the expedition, passed Finisterre without communicating with Calder, and having by this time got wind of their peril, they hurried into Lisbon, there to await developments in comparative safety, though their presence caused great embarrassment to the Portuguese Government and raised a diplomatic storm. It was not until Craig and Knight had ascertained that Villeneuve was out of the way and that Nelson had passed the Straits that they put to sea again and met Nelson off Cape St Vincent. Nelson had by this time satisfied himself, after an exhaustive survey of the situation, that Villeneuve had gone to the West Indies, and resolved to follow him there as soon as he had sped the expedition on its appointed way. But so apprehensive was he of

E

the Spanish ships remaining at Carthagena, that,
inferior to Villeneuve as he was, he detached the
" Royal Sovereign " from his own squadron, and
placed her under Knight's command. It only
remains to add that the expedition reached its destination in safety and that its result was the Battle
of Maida, fought in the following year—the first
battle in which Napoleon's troops crossed bayonets
with British infantry and were beaten by an inferior
force. The expedition was also the indirect cause
of the Battle of Trafalgar itself, for it was in order to
frustrate the coalition with Russia of which it was
the instrument that Napoleon had ordered Villeneuve
to make for the Mediterranean when he finally left
Cadiz to encounter Nelson on his path. Thus was it,
as Mr Corbett says, " to prove the insidious drop of
poison—the little sting—that was to infect Napoleon's
empire with decay and to force his hand with so
tremendous a result."

Yet it very nearly miscarried at the outset.
Nelson and Barham—between them a combination
of warlike energy and strategic insight, without a
parallel in the history of naval warfare—both
realized the tremendous risks it ran. It may be
argued that had Villeneuve gone to the north he
would have found himself in the thick of British
squadrons closing in on Brest and vastly superior
in force. Yet Allemand, who had escaped a few weeks

later from Rochefort, was able to cruise in these very waters for over five months without being brought to book. It is true that the destruction or capture of five thousand British troops would not seriously have affected the larger issues of the naval campaign, but it would have broken up the coalition with Russia by which Pitt set so much store, and which Mr Corbett at any rate represents as having exercised a decisive influence on the ultimate fortunes of Napoleon. The moral of the whole story seems to be that competent strategists—for the world has known none more competent and none more intrepid than Nelson and Barham—will not risk even a minor expedition at sea unless its line of advance is sufficiently controlled by superior naval force to ensure its unmolested transit. The principle thus exhibited in the case of a minor expedition manifestly applies with immensely increased force to those larger expeditions which assume the dimensions of an invasion. It was not until long after Trafalgar had been fought, and the command of the sea had been secured beyond the possibility of challenge, that the campaigns in the Peninsula were undertaken —campaigns which ended and were always intended to end, should the fortune of war so decree, in the invasion of France and the overthrow of Napoleon. This opens up the whole question of invasion, which will be discussed in the next chapter.

CHAPTER VI

ENGLAND has not been invaded since A.D. 1066, when, the country having no fleet in being, William the Conqueror effected a landing and subjugated the kingdom. During the eight centuries and more that have since elapsed, every country in Europe has been invaded and its capital occupied, in many cases more than once. It is by no means for lack of attempts to invade her that England has been spared the calamity of invasion for more than eight hundred years. It is not because she has had at all times—it may indeed be doubted if she has had at any time —organized military force sufficient to repel an invader, if he could not be stopped at sea. It is because she can only be invaded across the sea, and because whenever the attempt has been made she has always had naval force sufficient to bring the enterprise to nought. It is merely a truism to say that the invasion of hostile territory across the sea is a much more difficult and hazardous enterprise than the crossing of a land frontier by organized military force. But it is no truism to say that the reason why it is so much more difficult and more

68

hazardous is that there is no real parallel between
the two cases. I assume a vigorous defensive on
the part of the adversary assailed in both cases—
a defensive which, though commonly so called, is
really offensive in its nature. The essential difference
lies in this, that two countries which are separated
by the sea have no common frontier. Each has its
own frontier at the limit of its territorial waters,
but between these two there lies a region common
to both and from which neither can be excluded
except by the superior naval force of the other.

For the moment an expeditionary force emerges
from its own territorial waters—which may be any
distance from a few miles up to many thousands
of miles from the territorial waters of the adversary
to be assailed—it must be prepared to defend itself,
and naval force alone can afford it an adequate
measure of defence. Military forces embarked in
transports are defenceless and practically unarmed.
They cannot defend themselves with their own arms,
nor can the transports which carry them be so armed
as to afford adequate defence against the smallest
warship afloat, least of all against torpedo craft.
Hence, unless the sea to be traversed has been cleared
of the naval forces of the enemy beforehand, the
invading military force must be covered by a naval
force sufficient to overcome any naval force which
the enemy is able to bring against it. If the latter can

bring a fleet—as he must be able to do if the invasion is to be prevented—the covering fleet must be able to beat any fleet that he can bring. That condition being satisfied, however, it is clear that the covering fleet must be terribly hampered and handicapped in the ensuing conflict by the presence of a huge and unwieldy assemblage of unarmed transports filled with disarmed men, and by the consequent necessity of defending it against the attack of those portions of the enemy's naval force to which, albeit not suitable for engaging in the principal conflict, the transports would offer an otherwise defenceless prey. Hence the escorting fleet must be stronger than its adversary in a far larger proportion than it need be if naval issues pure and simple were alone at stake—so strong indeed that, if the transports were out of the way, its victory might be taken as certain. But if that is so it is manifest that the prospects of successful invasion would be immeasurably improved by seeking to decide the naval issue first—as Tourville very properly did in the Beachy Head campaign—and keeping the transports in hand and in port until it had been decided in favour of the intending invader. This is the eternal dilemma of invasion across a sea of which the command has not previously been secured. If you are not strong enough to dispose of the enemy's naval force you are certainly not strong enough to escort an invading force—itself helpless afloat—across the sea in his teeth. If you are strong enough to do this you will certainly be wise to beat him first, because then there will be nothing left to prevent the transit of your troops. In other words, command of the sea, if not absolutely and in all cases indispensable to a successful invasion, is at any rate the only certain way of ensuring its success.

Naval history from first to last is full of illustrations of the principles here expounded. I will examine one or two of them, and I must take my illustrations mainly from the naval history of Britain, first, because Britain, being an island, is the only country in Europe which cannot be invaded except across the sea, and secondly, because Britain for that very reason has often been subjected to attempts at invasion and has always frustrated them by denying to her adversary that sufficiency of sea control which, if history is any guide, is essential to successful invasion. But first I will examine two cases which might at first sight seem to militate against the principles I have enunciated. The brilliant campaign of Cæsar which ended in the overthrow of Pompey and his cause at Pharsalus, was opened by Cæsar's desperate venture of carrying his army across the Adriatic to the coast of Epirus, although Pompey's fleet was in full command of the waters traversed. This is one of those excep-

tions which may be said to prove the rule. Cæsar had
no alternative. Pompey was in Illyria, and if Cæsar
could not overthrow Pompey on that side of the
Adriatic it was certain that Pompey would overthrow
Cæsar on the other side. For this reason, and
perhaps for this reason alone, Cæsar was compelled
to undertake a venture which he must have known
to be desperate. How desperate it was is shown
by the fact that, not having transports enough to
carry more than half his army at once, he had to
send his transports back as soon as he had landed,
and they were all destroyed on their way back to
Brundusium. Antony his lieutenant did, indeed,
succeed after a time in getting the remainder of
his army across, but not before Cæsar had been
reduced to the utmost straits. The whole enterprise moreover was not, strictly speaking, an invasion of hostile territory. The inhabitants of the
territory occupied by both combatants were neutral
as between them, and were willing to furnish Cæsar
with such scanty supplies as they had. Again, an
army in those days needed no ammunition except
the sword which each soldier carried on his person,
and that kind of ammunition was not expended in
fighting. Hence Cæsar had no occasion to concern
himself with the security of his communications
across the sea—a consideration which weighs with
overwhelming force on the commander of a modern

oversea expedition. " A modern army," as the late Lord Wolseley said, " is such a complicated organism that any interruption in the line of communications tends to break up and destroy its very life." An army marches on its belly. If it cannot be fed it cannot fight. After the Battle of Talavera Wellington was so paralysed by the failure of the Spanish authorities to supply his troops with food that he had to abandon the offensive for a time and to retreat towards his own line of communication with the sea. Cæsar on the other hand abandoned the sea, which could not feed him, and trusted to the resources of the country. The difference is vital. The one risk that Cæsar ran was the destruction of his army afloat, and that he ran not because he chose but because he must. The risk of destruction on land he was prepared to run, and this, at any rate, was, as the event proved, a case of *bene ausus vana contemnere*.

Again, Napoleon's descent on Egypt is another exception which proves the rule, and proves it still more conclusively. Napoleon evaded Nelson's fleet and landed his army in Egypt. The army so landed left Egypt in British transports, having laid down its arms and surrendered just before the conclusion of the Peace of Amiens ; and but for the timely conclusion of that short-lived armistice, every French soldier who survived the Egyptian campaign might have seen the inside of a British

prison. This was because Napoleon, who never
fathomed the secrets of the sea, chose to think that
to evade a hostile fleet was the same thing as to
defeat it. He managed for a time to escape Nelson's
attentions by the skin of his teeth, and fondly fancied
that because he had done so the dominion of the East
was won. He was quickly undeceived by the
Battle of the Nile. That victory destroyed the fleet
which had escorted his army to Egypt and thereby
made it impossible for the army ever to return
except by consent of the Power which he never
could vanquish on the sea. The Battle of the Nile,
wrote a Frenchman in Egypt, " is a calamity which
leaves us here as children totally lost to the mother
country. Nothing but peace can restore us to her."
Nothing but the so-called Peace of Amiens did restore
them. If it be argued, as it often has been, that
Napoleon's successful descent on Egypt proves that
military enterprises of large moment may sometimes be undertaken without first securing the command of the sea to be traversed, surely the Battle
of the Nile and its sequel are a triumphant refuta-
tion of such an argument. Such enterprises are
merely a roundabout way of presenting the belligerent who retains the command of the sea with as
many prisoners of war as survive from the original
expedition.

I need not labour the point which the unbroken

testimony of history from the time of the Norman
Conquest has established, that all attempts to invade
England have been made in the past and must be
made in the future across a sea not commanded by
the intending invader. If he has secured the command of the sea beforehand, there is nothing to
prevent the invasion except the consideration that
he can attain his end—that is, the subjugation of the
nation's will—at less cost to himself. That being
premised, let us consider how the intending invader
will set about his task. There are three ways, and
three ways only. First, he may seek to overpower the
British naval defence on the seas, that is to obtain
the command of the sea. If he can do that, the
whole thing is done. Or secondly, he may collect
the military forces destined for the invasion in ports
suitable for the purpose, and when all is ready he
may cover their embarkation and transit by a naval
force sufficient to overcome any naval force which
this country can direct against it. I have already
shown, however, that a force sufficient to do this
with any certainty, or even with any reasonable
prospect of success, must needs be more than
sufficient to overpower the British naval defence
and thereby to secure the command of the sea, if
the enemy were freed from the entangling and wellnigh disabling necessity of providing for the safe
conduct of an unwieldy host of otherwise defenceless

transports. In other words he is putting the cart before the horse, a procedure which has never yet succeeded in getting the cart to its destination. This second alternative is then merely a clumsy and extremely inefficient way of attaining the same end as the first, and need only be mentioned in order to exclude it from further consideration.

There remains only a third alternative. This is to assemble the invading military force at suitable ports as before, and to attempt to engage the attention of the defending naval force by operations at a distance for a time sufficient to secure the unmolested transit of the military expedition. This is the method which has nearly always been employed by an enemy projecting an invasion of this country. It has never yet succeeded, because it always leads in the end to a situation which is practically indistinguishable from that involved in the second alternative, which I have already discussed and excluded. The naval and the military elements in the enterprise of invasion being now, by the hypothesis, separated in space and for that reason incapable of being very exactly combined in time, a whole series of highly indeterminate factors is thereby introduced into the problem to be solved by the invader. There are elements of naval force, to wit, all manner of small craft, which are not required for the main conflict of fleets—and it

is this conflict which alone can secure the command
of the sea—but which are eminently adapted for
the impeachment and destruction of unarmed transports. These will be employed in the blockade of
the ports in which the military forces are collecting.
If the assailant employs similar craft to drive the
blockaders away, the defender will bring up larger
craft to stiffen his blockading flotillas. The invading
force will therefore still be impeded and impeached.
The process thus goes on until, if it is not otherwise
decided by the conflict of the main fleets at a distance, the contending naval forces of both sides
are attracted to the scene of the proposed embarkation, there to fight it out in the conditions involved
in the second alternative considered above, conditions which I have already shown to be the least
favourable to the would-be invader. In a masterly
analysis Mr Julian Corbett has shown that the
British defence against a threatened invasion has
always been conducted on these lines, that the
primary objective of the defence has been the troops
and their transports, and that the vigorous pursuit
of this objective has always resulted in a decision
being obtained as between the main fleets of the two
belligerents. That the decision has always been in
favour of the British arms is at once a lesson and a
warning—a lesson that immunity from invasion can
only be ensured by superiority at sea, a warning

that such superiority can only be secured by the adequate preparation, the judicious disposition, and the skilful handling of the naval forces to be employed, as well as by an unflinching *animus pugnandi*. But no nation which goes to war can hope for more or be content with less than the opportunity of obtaining a decision in these conditions. The issue lies on the knees of the gods.

A few illustrations may here be cited. We have seen how in the Beachy Head campaign Tourville, having failed to force a decision on Torrington's fleet in being, could not turn aside with Torrington at his heels and Killigrew and Shovel on his flank to bring over an invading force from France. He was paralysed by that abiding characteristic of French naval strategy which impelled the French naval commanders to fix their eye on ulterior objects and blinded them to the fact that the best way to attain those objects was to destroy the naval forces of the enemy whenever the opportunity offered of so obtaining a decision. Hence their preference for the leeward position in action, their constant reluctance to fight a decisive action, their habitual direction of their fire at the masts and sails of the enemy rather than at his hulls, and in Tourville's case his failure to annihilate Torrington's fleet in being, resulting in the total miscarriage of the schemes for invasion, to be followed by internal insurrection, which, as Admiral Colomb has shown, were the kernel of the French plan of campaign. In the case of the Armada in the previous century, the task of invasion was entrusted to Parma, who had collected troops for the purpose, and vessels for their transport, in the ports of the Spanish Netherlands. But Justin of Nassau kept a close watch outside, and Parma could not move. He summoned Medina Sidonia with the Armada to his assistance, but he summoned him in vain, for the Armada, harassed throughout the Channel, and, as it were, smoked out of Calais, was finally shattered at Gravelines. Precisely the same thing happened in the eighteenth century during the Seven Years' War. Troops and transports were being collected in the Morbihan, but their exit was blocked by a British naval force stationed off the ports. Conflans with the French main fleet was at Brest, and there he was blockaded by Hawke. Evading the blockade, Conflans put to sea and straightway went to release the troops and transports, hopelessly blockaded in the Morbihan. But Hawke swooped down on him and destroyed him in Quiberon Bay, Boscawen having previously destroyed at Lagos the fleet which De La Clue was bringing from Toulon to effect a junction with Conflans.

One more illustration may be cited, and I will treat it at some length, because it presents certain

features which give it peculiar significance in re-
lation to current controversies. This is the projected invasion of England by France in 1744. It
is, so far as I know, the solitary instance in our
naval history which shows the enemy framing his
plans on the lines of what is now known as " a bolt
from the blue "—that is, he projected a surprise
invasion, at a time when the two countries were
nominally at peace, in the hope that the first overt
act of the war he was contemplating might be the
landing of his troops on British soil. In 1743, when
this project was conceived, England and France were,
as I have said, nominally at peace, but troops be-
longing to both had fought at Dettingen, not in
any direct quarrel of their own, but because England
was supporting Maria Theresa and France was supporting her enemies. The fleets of both Powers
were jealously watching each other in the Mediterranean, a situation which led early in 1744 to
the too notorious action of Mathews off Toulon.
Nevertheless, until the very end of 1743 no direct
conflict with France was anticipated by the English
Government.

Yet France was already secretly preparing
her " bolt from the blue." She had resolved
to support the Pretender's cause and to prepare
an invasion of England in which the Pretender's
son was to take part, and on landing in England

to rally his party to the overthrow of the Hanoverian dynasty. The bolt was to be launched from Dunkirk and directed at the Thames, the intention being to land the invading force at Blackwall. Some ten thousand French troops to be employed in the expedition were sent into winterquarters in and around Dunkirk, but this aroused no suspicion in England, because this region was the natural place for the left flank of the French army to winter in, and Dunkirk contained no transports at the time. Transports were, however, being taken up under false charter-parties at French ports on the Atlantic and in the Channel, and were ordered as soon as ready to rendezvous secretly and separately at Dunkirk. At first the intention was for the expeditionary force to make its attempt without any support from the French fleet. But Marshal Saxe, who was to command it and knew that the Thames and its adjacent waters were never denuded of naval force sufficient to make short work of a fleet of unarmed transports, flatly declined to entertain this project and demanded adequate nava support for the enterprise. Accordingly a powerful fleet, held to be sufficient to contain or defeat any British fleet that was thought likely to be able to challenge it, was fitted out with all secrecy at Brest and placed under the command of De Roquefeuil. Even he was not told its destination,

F

and false rumours on the subject were allowed to
circulate among those who were concerned in its
preparation.

So far everything seemed to be going well. The
blow was timed for the first week in January, but
the usual delays occurred, and for a month or more
after the date originally fixed, the expeditionary
force and its escort were separated by the whole
length of northern France. Yet even before the
date originally fixed, England had got wind of the
preparations. From the middle of December Brest
had been kept under watch, and orders had been
issued to the dockyards to prepare for sea as many
ships of the line as were available. These preparations were continued, without intermission, until the
end of January, the purpose and destination of the
armament at Brest still being unknown. Then two
alarming pieces of intelligence reached England at
the same time. One was that Roquefeuil had put
to sea on January 26 (O.S.) with twenty-one sail of
the line, and before being lost sight of by the British
cruiser told off to watch him, had been seen to be
clearly standing to the northward. The other was
that Prince Charles, the son of the Pretender, had
left Rome and had landed without hindrance in
France. This, being a direct violation of the Treaty
of Utrecht, was naturally held to give to the sailing
of the Brest fleet the complexion of a direct hostile

intent. It was on February 1 that these facts were
known, and on February 2, Sir John Norris, a
veteran of Barfleur and La Hogue, who was now
well over eighty years of age, but as the event showed
was still fully equal to the task entrusted to him,
was ordered to hoist his flag at Portsmouth and
to "take the most effectual measures to prevent
the making of any descent on the Kingdoms."
Norris hoisted his flag on the 6th, and by the 18th
he had eighteen sail of the line under his command.
Subsequently his force was increased to twenty.
Nothing was known of the movements of the French
fleet since January 29, when the frigate set to watch
it had finally lost sight of it. It was in fact still
off the mouth of the Channel, baffled by adverse
winds and gales and vainly seeking to make headway
against them. If it had gone to the Mediterranean,
Mathews off Toulon would be placed in grave
jeopardy, and there were some projects for detaching a powerful squadron of Norris's ships to his
support. If, on the other hand, it was aiming at
the Channel, Norris with his whole force would be
none too strong to encounter and defeat it. This
was Norris's dilemma, and it was not until February
9 that he learned from the Duke of Newcastle that
an embargo had been laid on all shipping at Dunkirk,
where some fifty vessels of one hundred and fifty to
two hundred tons had by this time assembled. These

might at a pinch and for a short transit be estimated
to be capable of transporting some ten thousand
troops. But an embargo, although clear proof of hostile intent, was not necessarily a sign of impending
invasion. It was a common expedient, preliminary
to war, whereby you deprived your enemy of ships
and men very necessary to his purposes and secured
ships and men equally necessary to your own. Hence
no strategic connexion could with any certainty
be held to exist between the embargo at Dunkirk
and the sailing of the French fleet from Brest.
On the other hand it was clearly dangerous to un-
cover the Channel so long as the destination of the
Brest fleet was unknown, and, although Newcastle
had suggested to Norris that he should divide his
fleet and send the major part of it to reinforce
Mathews in the Mediterranean, yet Norris strongly
demurred to the suggestion, and before the time
came to act on it the situation had so far developed
as to disallow it altogether. On February 11,
Norris received information that a French fleet
of at least sixteen sail of the line had been seen the
day before off the Start. This convinced him that
the French had some scheme to the eastward in
hand ; and as he had frigates watching the Channel
between the Isle of Wight and Cape Barfleur he was
equally convinced that the French had so far no
appreciable armed force to the eastward of him.

Newcastle, however, did not share this conviction. He had received numerous reports of movements of French ships in the Channel to the eastward of the Isle of Wight and other information which pointed to a concentration at Dunkirk. As a matter of fact no French men-of-war were at this time east of the Isle of Wight, and the vessels reported to Newcastle must have been transports making for Dunkirk and magnified into ships of the line by the fog of war. Newcastle, accordingly, ordered Norris to go forthwith to the Downs. Foul winds prevented Norris from sailing at once from St Helen's, and on the 13th, the day before he did sail, he received further information which confirmed his conviction that the French were still to the westward. But Newcastle's orders remained peremptory, and on the 14th he sailed with eighteen ships, and anchored in the Downs on the 17th. There he found two more ships awaiting him, while two others were on their way to join him from Plymouth.

I pause here for a moment to point out that Norris's desire, over-ruled by Newcastle, to remain at Portsmouth was thoroughly well advised. He knew that there was naval force enough in the Thames and the Downs to dispose of any expedition coming from Dunkirk unless it were escorted by the Brest fleet, or by a very considerable detachment

therefrom. He was well assured that no such
detachment could have eluded the vigilance of his
frigates, and he felt that in these circumstances he
could better impeach Roquefeuil by lying in wait
for him at Spithead or St Helen's than by preceding
him to the Downs. How right he was in this appreciation will be seen from a closer consideration of
the movements of the French fleet. It was not
until February 13 that Roquefeuil received his
final orders off the Start. He was directed to detach
De Baraille, his second in command, with five ships.
These were to go forthwith to Dunkirk and escort
Saxe's expedition, while he himself with the remainder of his fleet was to blockade Norris at
Portsmouth and defeat him if he could. But
Roquefeuil and his council of war found these orders
too hazardous for execution. They resolved not
to divide the fleet until at least Norris, presumed
to be at Portsmouth, had been disposed of. On
the 17th, the day on which Norris had anchored in
the Downs, they looked into Spithead and persuaded
themselves that they had seen Norris there with
eleven sail of the line. Judging that the weather
was too bad for a successful blockade, Roquefeuil
then passed on up the Channel, convinced that
Norris was now behind him with too weak a
force to be of any effect. Baraille was then sent
on with his detachment to Dunkirk, but by this

time Saxe had lost heart and declined to sail until Roquefeuil's whole fleet was at hand to escort him.

It never was at hand to escort him, and the expedition never sailed. Roquefeuil, with his fleet now greatly reduced, anchored off Dungeness on the 22nd, and never got any further. What had happened in the meanwhile was this. Norris remained in the Downs, being held there for some time by a gale. He was not unaware of what was going on at Dunkirk, but he hesitated to proceed thither lest the French fleet behind him should be covering another expedition coming from some French port in the Channel. He sent to reconnoitre, however, and on the 21st received information that four sixty-gun ships—these were, no doubt, Baraille's detachment—were at anchor off Gravelines, and there covering the transports at Dunkirk. On the 22nd, Roquefeuil appeared off Dungeness and anchored there. As soon as he knew Roquefeuil's whereabouts, Norris resolved to attack him without delay. The wind, being N.W., was favourable to his enterprise, and at the same time made it impossible for the expedition to leave Dunkirk. Should the wind change before Roquefeuil was brought to action and defeated, Norris held that he was strong enough to detach a force to impeach Saxe and Baraille, and at the same time to give a good account of Roquefeuil.

But matters did not exactly turn out in this wise. On the 24th Norris left the Downs, with a light wind from the N.W., and an ebb tide in his favour, making for Dungeness, where Roquefeuil was still lying. His appearance in the offing was Roquefeuil's first information that Norris was to the eastward of him in superior force, and it greatly disconcerted Roquefeuil. He held a hasty council of war and decided to cut and run. By this time the tide had turned and the wind had fallen, so that he could not stir until the tide again began to ebb. Norris, similarly disabled, had anchored some few miles to the eastward, intending to make his attack as soon as wind and tide allowed. But during the night a furious gale from the N.E. sprang up, which drove most of Norris's ships from their anchors, and when daylight came the French were nowhere to be seen. Roquefeuil had slipped his cables, and with the gale behind him was hurrying back to Brest. Norris went after him as far as Beachy Head, but there gave up the chase and returned to the Downs, to make sure that Saxe and Baraille, for whom the wind was now favourable, might find their way barred should they attempt to set sail. The transports, however, were by now in no position to move, nor was either Saxe or Baraille in any mind to allow them to move. They both realized that the game was up. The troops were in the transports, and they

suffered greatly in the gale that frustrated Norris'
attack on Roquefeuil. But that was merely an
accident of warfare. It was not the gale that
shattered the expedition, nor did it save England
from invasion. On the contrary, while it played
havoc with the transports and troops at Dunkirk,
it also saved Roquefeuil's fleet from destruction at
Dungeness. But, gale or no gale, the transports and
troops never could have crossed so long as Norris
held on to the Downs. Nor could they have crossed
had Norris been allowed to remain at Portsmouth as
he desired ; for in that case Baraille could not have
been detached.

To point the moral of this memorable story, I
cannot do better than quote Mr Julian Corbett's
comment on it. " The whole attempt, it will be
seen, with everything in its favour, had exhibited
the normal course of degradation. For all the
nicely framed plan and perfect deception, the inherent difficulties, when it came to the point of execution, had as usual forced a clumsy concentration
of the enemy's battle fleet with his transports,
and we on our part were able to forestall it with
every advantage in our favour by the simple expedient of a central mass on a revealed and certain
line of passage." We were certainly taken at a
disadvantage at the outset, for the " bolt from the
blue " was preparing some time before any one in

England got wind of it. The country had been largely denuded of troops for foreign enterprises, Scotland was deeply disaffected, the Jacobites were full of hope and intrigue, the Ministry was supine and feeble, the navy was deplorably weak in home waters, and such ships as were available had been dispersed to their ports for refit. Nevertheless with all these conditions in its favour the projected " bolt from the blue " was detected and anticipated— tardily, it is true, and with no great sagacity except on the part of Norris—long before the expedition was ready to start. Surely the moral needs no further pointing.

By these instances, and others which might be quoted, the law seems to be established that in default of an assured command of the sea the fleet which seeks to cover an invasion is drawn by irresistible attraction towards the place of embarkation, and that the same attraction brings it there —if not earlier—into conflict with the superior forces of the enemy. If in the Trafalgar campaign, which I have no space to examine in detail, the law does not seem to operate to the extent that it did in the other cases examined, that is only because the disposition of the British fleets was so masterly that Napoleon never got the opportunity he yearned for of bringing his fleets to the place of embarkation. They were outmanœuvred beforehand and finally overthrown at Trafalgar.

There is indeed a fourth alternative which has been advanced by some speculative writers, though history lends it no countenance, and it has never, I believe, been taken seriously by any naval authority of repute. I cannot take it seriously myself. It assumes that some naval Power, suitably situated as regards this country, might without either provocation or overt international dispute, clandestinely take up transport—either a comparatively small number of very large merchant vessels or a very large number of barges, lighters, or what not to be towed by steam vessels—might clandestinely put an army with all its necessary *impedimenta* on board the transports so provided and then clandestinely, and without either notice or warning, send them to sea, with or without escort, with intent to effect a landing at some suitable point on the English coast. The whole theory seems to me to involve at least three monstrous improbabilities : first, a piratical intent on the part of a civilized nation ; secondly, a concealment of such intent in conditions wellnigh incompatible with the degree of secrecy required ; and thirdly, a precision and a punctuality of movement in the operations of embarkation, transit, and landing of which history affords no example, while naval opinion and experience scoff at them as utterly impracticable. Of course the future may not resemble the past, and naval wars of the future may not be conducted on a pattern sealed by the unbroken teaching of over eight hundred years. But that is an assumption which I cannot seriously entertain.

CHAPTER VII

COMMERCE IN WAR

THE maritime trade of a nation at war has always
been regarded by the other belligerent as his legitimate prey. In the Dutch Wars the suppression
of the enemy's commerce was the main objective
of both parties to the conflict. In all wars in which
either belligerent has any commerce afloat worth
considering one belligerent may always be expected
to do all that he can for its capture or suppression,
while the other will do as much as he can for its
defence. In proportion to the volume and value
of the national trade afloat is the potency of its
destruction as an agency for bringing the national
will into submission. If, for example, the maritime trade of England could be suppressed by her
enemies, England would thereby be vanquished.
Her commerce is her life-blood. On the other hand
there are nations, very powerful in war, which
either by reason of their geographical position, or
because their oversea trade is no vital element in
their national economy, would suffer comparatively
little in like circumstances. It thus appears that
the volume and value of the national trade afloat

is the measure of the efforts which an enemy is likely to make for its suppression. But it is not directly the measure of the efforts which a nation so assailed must make for its defence. The measure of these efforts is determined not by the volume and value of the trade to be protected but by the amount and character of the naval force which the enemy can employ in assailing it. In the Boer War British maritime commerce was unassailed and uninterrupted in all parts of the world, and yet not a single ship of the British Navy was directly employed in its protection. If on the other hand England were at war with a naval Power of the first rank, she might have to employ the whole of her naval resources in securing the free transit of her maritime commerce. So long as she can do this with success she need give no thought to the menace of possible invasion. A command of the sea so far established as to secure freedom of transit for the vast and ubiquitous maritime commerce of this country is also, of necessity, so far established as to deny free transit to the transports of an enemy seeking to invade. The greater includes the less.

It may at first sight seem to be an anomaly—some, indeed, would represent it as a mere survival of barbarism—that whereas in war on land the private property of an enemy's subjects is, by the established law and custom of civilized nations, not liable to capture or destruction without compensation to its owners, the opposite rule still prevails in war at sea. But a little consideration will, I think, show that the analogy sought to be established between the two cases is a very imperfect one. War on land does *ipso facto* suspend in large measure the free transport of commerce in transit. As between the two belligerents it interrupts it altogether. Moreover, throughout the territory occupied by the enemy, the railways, and in large measure the roads, are practically monopolized for the movements of his troops and the transport of his supplies—in a word for the maintenance of his communications. There can have been little or no consignment of goods from Paris to Berlin or *vice versa* during the war of 1870, and even though at certain stages of the war goods might have been consigned, say, from Lyons to Geneva, or from Lille to Brussels, yet such cases are really only the counterparts of the frequent failure of one belligerent's cruisers to intercept the merchant vessels of the other on the high seas. Again, in the case of a beleaguered fortress, the besiegers would never dream of allowing a convoy of food or of munitions of war—or for the matter of that of merchandise of any kind—to enter the fortress. They would intercept it as a matter of course, and if necessary they would appropriate it to their own use. The

upshot of it all is that even in war on land the transit
of all commerce, albeit the private property of some
one, is practically suspended within the area of
the territory occupied, and very seriously impeded
throughout the whole country subject to invasion.
It is not, therefore, true to say without many qualifications that in war private property is respected
on land and not respected at sea. The only difference
that I can discern is that by the law and custom of
nations private property cannot be appropriated on
land, whereas at sea it can. But this difference is not
really essential. The essential thing in both cases
is that the wealth of the enemy is diminished and
the credit of his traders destroyed—a far more
important matter in these days than the destruction
of this or that cargo of his goods—by the suspension
of that interchange of commodities with other
nations which is the chief element of national pro-
sperity, and may be, as in the case of England,
the indispensable condition of national existence.
Indeed, although private property on land is exempt
from capture, and at sea it is not, yet there are
many nations which would suffer far more from the
interruption of their mercantile communications
which war on land entails than they would from the
destruction of their commerce at sea.

For these reasons I hold that the proposed exemp-
tion of private property from capture or molestation

at sea is a chimerical one. War is essentially an
act of violence. It operates by the destruction of
human life as well as by all other agencies which
are likely to subdue the enemy's will. Among these
agencies the capture or destruction of commerce
afloat is by far the most humane since it entails the
least sacrifice of life, limb, or liberty, and at the
same time its coercive pressure may in some cases,
though not in all, be the most effective instrument
for compelling the enemy's submission. Moreover, it
is not proposed to exempt from capture or destruction such merchant vessels of the enemy—or even
of a neutral for that matter—as attempt to break a
blockade. Now the modern conditions of blockade
are such that the warships conducting it may be
stationed hundreds of miles from the blockaded
port or ports, and their outlying cruisers, remaining
in touch with each other and with the main body,
may be much further afield. Within the area of
the organized patrol thus established, every vessel
seeking to enter a blockaded port or to issue from it
will still be liable to capture. In these conditions
the proposal to exempt the remainder of the enemy's
private property afloat from capture would be a
mockery. There would not be enough of such
property afloat to pay for the cost of capture.

It is an axiom of naval warfare that an assured
command of the sea is at once the best defence

G

for commerce afloat and an indispensable condition
for any such attack on it as is likely to have any
appreciable effect in subduing the enemy's will.
War is an affair not of pin-pricks but of smash-
ing blows. "The harassment and distress," says
Admiral Mahan, "caused to a country by serious
interference with its commerce will be conceded by
all. It is doubtless a most important secondary
operation of naval war, and is not likely to be
abandoned until war itself shall cease ; but regarded as a primary and fundamental measure
sufficient in itself to crush an enemy, it is probably
a delusion, and a most dangerous delusion, when
presented in the fascinating garb of cheapness to
the representatives of a people." Here again we
may discern some of the larger implications of that
potent and far-reaching agency of naval warfare,
the command of the sea. If a belligerent not aiming
at the command of the sea, and having no sufficient
naval force wherewithal to secure it, thinks to crush
his enemy by directing sporadic attacks on his
commerce, he will, if history is any guide, soon
find out his mistake. His naval forces available
for this purpose, are, by the hypothesis, inferior to
those of the enemy. It is certain that they will
sooner or later be hunted down and destroyed.
Moreover, the mercantile flag of the weaker belligerent will, as I have shown, disappear from the sea

from the very outset of the conflict ; and the maritime commerce of such a belligerent must be of very insignificant volume if the loss entailed by its suppression is not greater than that likely to be inflicted by such a belligerent on the enemy's commerce which crosses the seas under the *ægis* of a flag which commands them. Admiral Mahan has estimated that during the whole of the war of the French Revolution and Empire the direct loss to England "by the operation of hostile cruisers did not exceed 2½ per cent. of the commerce of the Empire ; and that this loss was partially made good by the prize ships and merchandise taken by its own naval vessels and privateers." It should be noted, however, that the Royal Commission on Food Supply was of opinion that 4 per cent. would be a more accurate estimate. It is also well known that during the same period the maritime commerce of England was doubled in volume while that of France was annihilated. In point of fact the risks run in war by commerce afloat are measured very exactly by the degree in which the flag which covers it has secured the command of the sea—that is, be it always remembered, the control of the maritime communications affected. During the War of American Independence, when British supremacy at sea was seriously challenged and at times was in grave jeopardy—owing quite as much to faulty disposition as to inferiority of force—premiums of fifteen guineas per cent. were paid in 1782 on ships trading to the Far East ; whereas from the spring of 1793 until the close of the struggle with Napoleon no premiums exceeding half that rate were paid. Yet to the very end of the war British merchant vessels were being seized even in the Channel almost every day. There is, however, good reason to think that many of these seizures were in reality collusive operations undertaken for the purpose of carrying on clandestinely the direct trade with the Continent which Napoleon sought in vain to suppress. The full history of the memorable conflict between the Berlin Decrees of Napoleon and the British Orders in Council, is still to be written. Some very illuminating sidelights are thrown on it by Mr David Hannay in a volume entitled *The Sea-Trader, His Friends and Enemies*.

It would seem to follow from these premisses— fortified as they are by other historical examples that might be cited—that of two belligerents in a naval war, that one which establishes and maintains an effective command of the sea will be absolute master of the maritime commerce of the other, while his own maritime commerce, though not entirely immune, will suffer no such decisive losses as will determine or even materially affect the course and issue of the war; and that he may indeed emerge from the war much stronger and more prosperous than he was at the beginning. Such is assuredly the teaching of history, and although vast changes have taken place alike in respect of the methods, opportunities, implements, and international conventions of naval war and in respect of the conditions, volume, and national importance of maritime commerce, yet I think it can be shown that the sum total of these changes has made on the whole rather for the advantage of the superior belligerent than otherwise. In the first place privateering—formerly a very effective weapon in the hands of the weaker belligerent—is now abolished. It is true that the Declaration of Paris, which recorded and ratified its abolition, has not been formally accepted by all the naval Powers of the world; but it is also true that since its promulgation no naval Power has sought to revive privateering. It is indeed held by some that the right claimed by certain maritime Powers to convert merchant ships of their own nationality into warships by arming and commissioning them on the high seas is, or may be, equivalent to the revival of privateering in its most dangerous and aggressive form. But those who argue thus appear to overlook the fact that this process of conversion on the high seas is by the Seventh Convention of the Second

Hague Conference hedged round with a series of restrictions which differentiate the warship thus improvised very sharply from the privateer of the past. The following are the leading provisions of this Convention :—

1. A merchant ship converted into a warship cannot have the rights and duties appertaining to vessels having that status unless it is under the direct authority, immediate control, and responsibility of the Power the flag of which it flies.

2. Merchant ships converted into warships must bear the external marks which distinguish the warships of their nationality.

3. The commander must be in the service of the State and duly commissioned by the proper authorities. His name must figure on the list of the officers of the fighting fleet.

4. The crew must be subject to military discipline.

5. Every merchant ship converted into a warship is bound to observe in its operations the laws and customs of war.

6. A belligerent who converts a merchant ship into a warship must, as soon as possible, announce such conversion in the list of its warships.

This Convention has been accepted and ratified by all the great maritime Powers. It is true that it gives the converted merchant ship what may be called the dog's privilege of taking a first bite with impunity, but it makes it very difficult for any second bite to be taken. Such a vessel may as a merchant ship have obtained coal and other supplies in a neutral port before conversion, but she cannot after conversion return to the same or another neutral port and repeat the process ; nor can she easily play the game which some have attributed to her of being a merchant ship one day, a warship the next, and a merchant ship again on the third. Further, as a weapon to be employed against England in particular, the method of conversion here prescribed would seem to be largely discounted by the fact that this country could, if it were so disposed, convert as many merchant ships into warships in this way as all the rest of the world put together.

It will be argued, perhaps, that a belligerent when hard pressed will not respect the provisions of a mere paper Convention, but will, if it suits him, treat them as non-existent. In that case it is not easy to see why he should ever have accepted and ratified them. The preamble of this very Convention recites that " whereas the contracting Powers have been unable to come to an agreement on the question whether the conversion of a merchant ship into a warship may take place upon the high seas, it is understood that the question of the place where such conversion is effected remains outside the scope of this agreement, and is in no way affected by the following rules." In other words some of the very Powers which have ratified the Convention as it stands categorically declined to add to it a provision forbidding altogether the conversion of a merchant ship into a warship on the high seas. If this does not mean that, while reserving their freedom of action in this respect, they are prepared to abide by the provisions of a Convention which they have not less categorically accepted and ratified we are driven to the absurd conclusion that all International Law is a nullity.

Secondly, the practical disappearance of the sailing ship from the seas has profoundly modified all the pre-existing conditions affecting the attack and defence of commerce afloat. In the days of sailing, all vessels were compelled to sail according to the wind, that is, to take devious courses whenever the wind was adverse, so that some of them might at all times be found scattered over very wide areas of the seas connecting the ports of departure with those of arrival. Accordingly the sporadic attack on commerce by isolated warships cruising at large within the limits of trade routes, which might be hundreds of miles in width, was often productive of very appreciable results. There were few blank coverts on the seas to be drawn. Nowadays a steamer can always take the most direct course to her destination. As a consequence, trade routes have now been narrowed down to what may more fittingly be called lines of communication, and these lines possess the true characteristic of all lines, namely, that they have practically no breadth. Thus the areas bounded by these lines are nowadays all blank coverts. Any one who happens to cross the Atlantic, as I have crossed it more than once, by one of the less frequented routes, will know that the number of vessels sighted in a voyage quite as long as any warship could take without coaling may often be counted on the fingers of one hand. Another characteristic of these lines is that though their points of departure and destination are fixed, yet the lines joining these points may be varied if necessary to such an extent that any warship hovering about their ordinary direction would be thrown entirely off the scent. On the other hand their ports of departure and destination being fixed, the lines of communication must inevitably converge as they approach these points. There are other points also more in the open at which several lines of communication may intersect. At these "terminal and focal points," as Mr Corbett has aptly called them, the belligerent, being by hypothesis inferior to his adversary, must needs endeavour to concentrate his attack on his enemy's commerce, because at any other points the game would not be worth the candle.

But it is precisely at these points that the superior adversary will concentrate his defence, and being superior, will take care to do so in force sufficient for the purpose. So far as the remaining portions of the lines of communication need any direct defence at all this can be afforded, if and when necessary, by collecting the merchant ships about to traverse them into convoys and giving them an escort sufficiently powerful to deal effectually with attacks which from the nature of the case can only be sporadic and intermittent. Be it remembered that the last thing a warship bent on commerce destruction wants is to encounter an enemy in superior or even in equal force. The moment she does so her game is up.

Thirdly, the substitution of steam for sails has very largely reduced the enduring mobility of the commerce-destroying warship. In time of war no warship will ever go further from the nearest available supply of coal than is represented by considerably less than half of the distance that she can steam at full speed with her bunkers full. If she does so she runs the risk, if chased, of burning her last pound of coal before she has reached shelter. Coaling at sea is only possible in exceptional circumstances, and is in any case a very tedious operation. A warship which attempts it will be taken at a great disadvantage if an enemy catches her in the process. Colliers, moreover, are exposed to capture while proceeding to the appointed rendezvous, and if they fail to reach it the warship awaiting them will be placed in extreme danger. All these difficulties and dangers may be surmounted once and again, but they must needs put a tremendous handicap in the long run on the commerce-destroying efforts of a belligerent who is not superior to his adversary at sea. Of course if he is superior at sea the enemy's commerce will be at his mercy, and nothing can prevent its destruction or at least its total suppression. But that is not the hypothesis we are considering.

Fourthly, the power of the modern warship to send her prizes into court for adjudication, or to destroy them off-hand on capture is much more limited than was that of her sailing predecessor. If she sends them into port she must either put a prize crew on board or escort them herself. In the former case the prizes, and in the latter case both prizes and their captors are liable to recapture, a liability which becomes the greater in proportion as the enemy is superior at sea. As to the former alternative, moreover, the crew of a modern man-of-war is highly specialized, and in particular its engine-room complement, which must furnish a portion of every prize crew, is at the outset no greater than is required for the full fighting efficiency of the ship. It is probable, therefore, that the captor would in nearly all cases adopt the alternative of destroying his prizes at sea. In that case there will be no prize money for any one concerned, but that is perhaps a minor consideration. A far more important consideration is that before destroying the prize the captor must take its crew on board and provide food and accommodation for them. Any other course would be sheer piracy and would inevitably lead to drastic reprisals. Now, before the captor had destroyed many prizes in this fashion—especially if even one of them happened to be a passenger steamer well filled with passengers—she would find herself gravely embarrassed by the number of her prisoners, and the need of providing for them even in the roughest fashion. A captain having to fight his ship even with a few hundreds of prisoners on board would be in no very enviable position.

The foregoing are the leading considerations which appear to me to govern the problem of the attack and defence of maritime commerce in modern conditions of naval warfare. I have discussed the question in greater detail in a work entitled *Nelson and Other Naval Studies*, and as I have seen no reason to abandon or substantially to modify the conclusions there formulated, I reproduce them here for the sake of completeness :—

1. All experience shows that commerce-destroying never has been, and never can be, a primary object of naval war.

2. There is nothing in the changes which modern times have witnessed in the methods and appliances of naval warfare to suggest that the experience of former wars is no longer applicable.

3. Such experience as there is of modern war points to the same conclusion and enforces it.

4. The case of the " Alabama," rightly understood, does not disallow this conclusion but rather confirms it.

5. Though the volume of maritime commerce has vastly imcreased, the number of units of naval force capable of assailing it has decreased in far greater proportion.

6. Privateering is, and remains abolished, not merely by the fiat of International Law, but by changes in the methods and appliances of navigation and naval warfare which have rendered the privateer entirely obsolete.

7. Maritime commerce is much less assailable than in former times, because the introduction of steam has confined its course to definite trade routes of extremely narrow width, and has almost denuded the sea of commerce outside these limits.

8. The modern commerce destroyer is confined to a comparatively narrow radius of action by the inexorable limits of her coal supply. If she destroys her prizes she must forgo the prize money and find accommodation for the crews and passengers of

the ships destroyed. If she sends them into port she must deplete her engine-room complement and thereby gravely impair her own efficiency.

9. Torpedo craft are of little or no use for commerce destruction except in certain well-defined areas where special measures can be taken for checking their depredations.

Of course all this depends on the one fundamental assumption that the commerce to be defended belongs to a Power which can, and does, command the sea. On no other condition can maritime commerce be defended at all.

CHAPTER VIII

A WARSHIP, considered in the abstract, may be defined as a vessel employed, and generally constructed, for the purpose of conveying across the seas to the place of conflict, the weapons that are to be used in conflict, the men who are to use them, and all such stores, whether of food or other supplies, as will give to the vessel as large a measure of enduring mobility as is compatible with her displacement. If we confine our attention to the period posterior to the employment of the gun on shipboard as the principal weapon of offence, and if we regard the torpedo as a particular kind of projectile, and the tube from which it is discharged as a particular kind of gun, we may condense this definition into the modern formula that a warship is a floating gun-carriage. With the methods and implements of sea warfare anterior to the introduction of the gun we need not concern ourselves. They belong to the archæology of the subject. It suffices to point out that in all periods of naval warfare the nature of the principal weapon employed, and to some extent that of the motive power available, have not only governed the structure of the ship and determined the practicable limit of its displacement, but have also exercised a dominant influence over the ordering of fleets and their disposition in action. Sea tactics have never been more elaborate than they were in the last days of the galley period which came to an end with the Battle of Lepanto in 1571, less than a score of years before the defeat of the Armada in 1588. But the substitution of sails for oars as the motive power of the warship and the more general employment of the gun as the principal weapon of offence necessarily entailed radical changes in the tactical methods which had been slowly evolved during the galley period. At first all was confusion and a sea-fight was reduced for a time to a very disorderly and tumultuous affair. " We went down in no order," wrote an officer who was present at Trafalgar, " but every man to take his bird." This is a very inaccurate and even more unintelligent account of the tactics pursued at Trafalgar ; but it might very well stand for a picturesque summary of the tactical confusion which prevailed at the period of the Armada and for half a century afterwards.

Gradually, however, order was again evolved out of the prevailing chaos. But it was not the old order. It was a new order based on the predominance of the gun and its disposition on board the ship. To go down in no order and for each man to take his bird would mean that each ship, whether large or small, would be free as far as circumstances permitted to select an adversary not disproportioned in strength to herself, so that there was no very pressing need for the fleet to consist of homogeneous units, nor for the elimination of comparatively small craft from a general engagement. But in the course of the Dutch Wars the practice was slowly evolved of fighting in a compact or close-hauled line, the ships being ranged in a line ahead—that is, each succeeding ship following in the wake of her next ahead—in order to give free play to the guns disposed mainly on the broadside, and being, for purposes of mutual support, disposed as closely to each other as was compatible with individual freedom of evolution and manœuvre. This disposition necessarily involved the exclusion from the line of battle of all vessels below a certain average or standard of fighting strength, since it was no longer possible for "every man to take his bird" and a weak ship might find herself in conflict with an adversary of overpowering strength in the enemy's line. Hence the main fighting forces of naval belligerents came in time to be composed entirely of "ships fit to lie in a line," as Torrington phrased it, of "capital ships," as they were frequently called in former days, of "line of battle ships"

H

or " ships of the line," as afterwards they were more
commonly called, or of " battleships " as is nowadays the accepted appellation. Other elements
of naval force not " fit to lie in a line " were also
required, as I am about to show, and took different
forms at different times, but the root of the whole
evolution lies in the elimination of the non-capital
ship from the main fighting line. In a very instructive chapter of his *Naval Warfare*, Admiral
Colomb has traced the whole course of this gradual
" Differentiation of Naval Force." But for my
purpose it suffices to cite the briefer exposition
of a French writer quoted by Admiral Mahan in
his *Influence of Sea Power upon History* :—

" With the increase of the power of the ship of
war, and with the perfecting of its sea and warlike
qualities, there has come an equal progress in the
art of utilizing them. . . . As naval evolutions
become more skilful, their importance grows from
day to day. To these evolutions there is needed
a base, a point from which they depart and to which
they return. A fleet of warships must always be
ready to meet an enemy ; logically, therefore, this
point of departure for naval evolutions must be the
order of battle. Now since the disappearance of
galleys, almost all the artillery is found upon the
sides of a ship of war. Hence it is the beam that
must necessarily and always be turned toward the

enemy. On the other hand it is necessary that the sight of the latter must never be interrupted by a friendly ship. Only one formation allows the ships of the same fleet to satisfy fully these conditions. That formation is the line ahead. The line, therefore, is imposed as the only order of battle, and consequently as the basis of all fleet tactics. In order that this line of battle, this long thin line of guns, may not be injured or broken at some point weaker than the rest, there is at the same time felt to be the necessity of putting in it only ships which, if not of equal force, have at least equally strong sides. Logically it follows, at the same moment in which the line ahead became definitely the order for battle, there was established the distinction between the 'ships of the line' alone destined for a place therein, and the lighter ships meant for other uses."

But the need for other and lighter ships " meant for other uses " and not " fit to lie in a line," is equally demonstrable. The function of battleships is to act in concert. They must therefore be concentrated in fleets sufficiently strong to give a good account of the enemy's fleets opposed to them. This does not necessarily mean that all the fleets of a belligerent must be concentrated in a single position. But it does mean that if disposed in accordance with the dispositions of the enemy they must be so disposed and connected, that, moving on interior lines, they can always bring a superior force to the point of contact with the enemy. Subject to this paramount condition, that of being able to concentrate more rapidly than the enemy can, dispersal of naval force—not of units but of organized fighting fleets—is generally a better disposition than extreme concentration. But it is a fatal error in strategy so to disperse your fleets as to expose them to the risk of being overpowered by the enemy in detail.

The fleets of capital ships thus organized, and disposed as occasion may require and sound strategy dictate, are not, however, by any means to be regarded as autonomous and self-sufficing organisms. They are rather to be regarded as the moving base of a much larger organization, much more widely dispersed, consisting of lighter vessels not fit to lie in a line, but specially adapted to discharge functions which capital ships cannot as such discharge, yet which are indispensable either to the full efficiency of the latter or to the maintenance of an effective command of the sea. The first of these functions is the collection and rapid transmission of intelligence as to the enemy's dispositions and movements over as wide an area of the waters in dispute as is compatible with communication rapid enough to allow of counter-movements being made before it is too late. The development of wireless telegraphy has largely extended this area, but it is not without limits in practice, and those limits are already narrower than the extreme range of a single transmission by wireless telegraphy. For example, a warship in the Levant might, if the conditions were exceptionally favourable, communicate by direct wireless with another warship in the Orkneys. But the information thus transmitted would hardly be likely directly to influence the movements and dispositions of the latter. If it did it would probably not be through the immediate initiative of the Admiral commanding in the North Sea, but through the supreme control of all the naval forces of the belligerent affected, exercised through the General Staff of the Navy at the seat of Government. It may here be remarked in passing that the development of wireless telegraphy will probably be found in war to strengthen this supreme control and to weaken to that extent the independent and isolated initiative of individual Commanders-in-Chief. But that is not necessarily a disadvantage, and even so far as it is disadvantage at all it is more than balanced by the immense corresponding advantage of keeping the War Staff at all times in direct touch with every part of the field of naval operations, and thereby making it the focus of all available information, and the directing authority for all the

larger strategy of the campaign.   Except in degree,
moreover, there is nothing new in this.   When
Nelson was returning across the Atlantic, after
chasing Villeneuve out of the West Indies, his only
way of informing the Admiralty of the nature of the
situation was to send on Bettesworth in the brig
" Curieux " with his news.   Nowadays a modern
" Curieux " would be able to send on the news as soon
as she came within fifteen hundred or possibly two
thousand miles from the British Isles, and Nelson
at the same distance might have received his orders
direct from the Admiralty.   But the special point
to note is that as soon as Bettesworth's information
was received at the Admiralty, Barham, the First
Lord of the Admiralty, instantly issued orders which
profoundly modified the dispositions of the fleets
engaged in blockading the French ports and led
directly to Calder's action off Finisterre, and in the
sequel to the abandonment by Napoleon of all his
projects of invasion and the destruction of the allied
fleets at Trafalgar.   There were giants in those days
both afloat and ashore.   But the giants afloat did
not resent the interference of the giants ashore, and,
as Mr Corbett has shown, the Trafalgar campaign
was conducted with consummate sagacity by
Barham, who embodied in himself the War Staff
of the time.

Such is the transcendent importance of intelligence, and of its collection, transmission, collation, interpretation, and translation into supreme executive orders. Its collection and transmission is mainly the function of cruising ships disposed either individually or in small groups for the purpose, and at such a distance from the main body of battleships as is not incompatible with the movements of the latter being controlled and directed, either by their immediate commanders, or by the War Staff at the centre, according to the information received from the outlying cruisers. Such cruising vessels may vary in size and strength from the modern battle-cruiser, so heavily armed and armoured as to be not incapable of taking a place, on occasion, in the line of battle, down to the smallest torpedo craft which is endowed with sufficient enduring mobility to enable her to keep the sea and to cruise as near as may be to the enemy's ports. I have already indicated the other collateral functions which will have to be discharged by torpedo craft in case of a blockade and pointed out the vital distinction which differentiates them from the small craft of the past in that in certain circumstances they are capable of taking a formidable part in a fleet action even as against the most powerful battleships. But we are here considering them solely from the point of view of their cruising functions, whether as guarding their own shores or watching those of the enemy with a view to fighting on occasion and to observation at all times. Their supports will be cruisers of larger size, disposed at suitable distances in the rear, and themselves supported in like manner by successive cordons or patrols of cruisers increasing in size and power, until we come to the battle fleet as the concentrated nucleus of the whole organization. This is merely an abstract or diagrammatic exposition of such an organization, and it is of course liable to almost infinite variation in the infinite variety of warlike operations at sea, but it serves to exhibit the *rationale* of the differentiation of naval force into battleships, cruisers, and small craft.

It has sometimes been argued that, inasmuch as the torpedo craft is, or may be, in certain conditions, more than a match for even the biggest battleship, battleships together with all intermediate ships between the battleship and the torpedo vessel, are not unlikely to be some day regarded as superfluous and in consequence to be discarded altogether from the naval armament of even a first-class maritime Power. It is true that the range and accuracy of the torpedo have latterly undergone an immense development, so that a range of even ten thousand yards or five sea-miles is no longer beyond its powers. It is true that the development of the submarine vessel has vastly intensified the menace of the torpedo and it may soon be true that the development of aircraft will add a new and very formidable menace to the supremacy of the battleship. But except for this last consideration, which is at present exceedingly speculative, a little reflection will disclose the underlying fallacy of arguments of this kind. The enduring mobility of the torpedo craft is necessarily limited. It is incapable of that wide range of action which is required of warships if they are to establish and maintain any effective command of the sea. It is exceedingly vulnerable to ships of a larger size, and of more ample enduring mobility. These again will be vulnerable in their turn to ships of a still larger size and thus the logic of the situation brings us back to the battleship once more with its characteristic functions. It may perhaps be urged that this chain of argument takes too little account of the submarine vessel which is at present singularly invulnerable because for the most part invisible to any vessels, whether big or little, which operate only on the surface and even if discovered betimes by the latter, is not very readily assailable by them. But of two things one. Either the submarine vessel will remain small and therefore weak, and lacking in enduring mobility, in which case it can never establish and maintain an effective command of the sea. Or it will grow indefinitely in size, in which case it will fall under the inexorable stress of the logic which brings us back once more to the battleship. It may be that the battleship of the still distant future will be a submersible battleship. But many exceedingly complex problems of construction and stability will have to be solved before that consummation is reached.

Lastly, the specific function of the so-called battle-cruiser would seem to need some further elucidation. At first sight this hybrid type of vessel might seem to be an anomalous intrusion into the time-honoured hierarchy of battleship, cruiser, and small craft, which the ripe experience of many wars, battles, and campaigns had finally established in the last golden days of the sailing ship period. It is indeed held by some high authorities that the battle-cruiser is in very truth a hybrid and an anomaly, and that no adequate reason for its existence can be given. In face of these opinions I cannot presume to dogmatize on the subject. But some not wholly irrelevant considerations may be advanced. The battle-cruiser is, as its name implies, a vessel not only fitted by the nature of its armour and armament " to lie in a line," whenever occasion may require, but also exceedingly well qualified by its armour and armament, and still more by its speed, to discharge many of the functions of a cruiser either alone or in company with other cruisers. In this latter capacity, it can overhaul nearly every merchant ship afloat, it can scout far and wide, it can push home a vital reconnaissance in cases where a weaker and slower cruiser would have to run away if she could, it can serve as a rallying point to a squadron of smaller cruisers engaged in the defence of this or that vital line of communication, and alone or in company with a consort of the same type it can hold the terminal and focal points of any such line against almost any number of hostile cruisers inferior in defensive and offensive powers to itself. Such are its powers and capacities when acting as a cruiser proper. But it may be thought that in the stress of conflict it will have very little opportunity of displaying these very exceptional powers because an admiral in command of a fighting fleet will never, when anticipating an engagement with the enemy, consent to weaken his fighting line by detaching so powerful a unit for scouting or other cruising purposes. That is as it may be. It will depend on many circumstances of the moment not to be clearly anticipated or defined beforehand ; on the strength of the enemy's force, on the personality, sagacity, and fortitude of the admiral—whether he is or is not a man of the mettle and temper ascribed to Nelson by Admiral Mahan in a passage already quoted— on the comparative need as determined by the circumstances of the moment of scouting for information, of cruising for the defence of trade, or of strengthening the battle line for a decisive conflict to the uttermost extent of the nation's resources. It is unbecoming to assume that in the crisis of his country's fate an admiral will act either as a fool or as a poltroon. It is the country's fault if a man capable of so acting is placed in supreme command, and for that there is no remedy. But it is sounder to assume that the admiral selected for command is a man not incapable of disposing his force to the best advantage. "We must," said Lord Goschen, on one occasion, "put our trust in Providence and a good admiral." If a nation cannot find a good admiral in its need it is idle to trust in Providence.

It remains to consider the function of the battle-cruiser in the line of battle. The lines of battle in former times were often composed of ships of varying size and power. There was a legitimate prejudice against ships of excessive size, although their superior power in action was recognized— we have the unimpeachable testimony on that point of Nelson's Hardy, a man of unrivalled fighting experience to whom Nelson himself attributed " an intuitive right judgment "—because they were unhandy in manœuvre and slow in sailing as compared with ships of more moderate dimensions. But except for difficulties of docking—a very serious

consideration from the financial point of view—
hardly any limit can be assigned to the size of the
modern warship on these particular grounds.   Quite
the contrary.   Other things being equal, the bigger
the ship the higher the speed, and it is well known
that ships of the Dreadnought type are as handy to
steer as a torpedo boat.   For tactical reasons,
moreover, it is not expedient to lengthen the line
of battle unduly.   Hence there is a manifest advantage in concentrating offensive power, as far as
may be, in single units.   On the other hand, the
experience and practice of the eighteenth century
showed conclusively that there was also a distinct
advantage in having in the line of battle a certain
number of ships which, being smaller than their
consorts were more handy and faster sailing than
the latter.   The enemy might not want to fight.
Very often he did not, and by crowding all possible
sail he did his best to get away.   In this case the
only way to bring him to action was for the pursuing admiral to order " a general chase "—that is,
to direct his ships, disregarding the precise line of
battle, to hurry on with all possible sail after the
enemy so that the fastest ships of the pursuing fleet
might bring individually to action the laggards
of the retreating fleet and hold them until the main
body of the pursuing fleet came up.   In this case
the retreating admiral must either return to the

succour of his ships astern and thereby accept the general action which he sought to avoid, or abandon his overtaken ships to the enemy without attempting to rescue them. Hawke's action in Quiberon Bay and Duncan's action off Camperdown are two of the most memorable examples of this particular mode of attack, and their brilliant results are a striking testimony to its efficacy. If ever in the naval battles of the future it becomes expedient for an admiral to order a general chase, it stands to reason that ships of the battle-cruiser type will be invaluable for the purpose. Their speed will enable them to hold the tail of the enemy's line, and their power will enable them to crush it unless the retreating admiral who seeks to avoid a decisive action turns back to succour such of his ships as are assailed and thereby renders a decisive action inevitable.

There is, moreover, another function to be assigned to the battle-cruiser in a general action, and that is a function which was defined once for all by Nelson himself in the immortal memorandum in which he explained to his captains the mode of attack he proposed to carry out at Trafalgar. " I have," wrote Nelson, " made up my mind to keep the fleet in that position of sailing . . . that the order of sailing is to be the order of battle, placing the fleet in two lines of sixteen ships each, with an advanced squadron of eight *of the fastest sailing two-decked ships* which will always make, if wanted, a line of twenty-four sail, on whichever line the Commander-in-Chief may direct." Owing to the lack of ships this disposition was not adopted on the day of Trafalgar, but the principle involved is not affected by that circumstance. That principle is that a squadron of the fastest sailing ships in the fleet was to be detached from the two fighting lines entrusted with the initial attack, and reserved or " refused " until the development of the main attack had disclosed to the Commander-in-Chief the point at which the impact of this " advanced squadron " would by superior concentration on that point secure that the enemy should there be decisively overpowered. The essence of the matter is that the ships so employed should by virtue of their superior speed be endowed with a tactical mobility sufficient to enable them to discharge the function assigned to them. I need hardly insist on the close analogy which subsists between Nelson's " advanced squadron " and a modern squadron of battle-cruisers similarly employed, and although the conflict of modern warships must needs differ in many essential respects from the conflicts of sailing ships in Nelson's days, yet I think a clear and authoritative exposition of one at least of the uses and functions of the battle-cruiser in a fleet action may still be found in what I have called elsewhere " the last tactical word of the greatest master of sea tactics the world has ever known, the final and flawless disposition of sailing ships marshalled for combat."

CHAPTER IX

THE measure of naval strength required by any State is determined mainly by the naval strength of its possible adversaries in the event of war, and only in a secondary degree by the volume of the maritime interests which it has to defend. Paradoxical as the latter half of this proposition may seem at first sight, it can easily be shown to be sound. The maritime interests, territorial and commercial, of the British Empire are beyond all comparison greater than those of any other State in the world ; but if no other State possessed a naval force strong enough to assail them seriously, it is manifest that the naval force required to defend them need be no greater than is sufficient to overcome the assailant, and would not therefore be determined in any degree by the volume of the interests to be defended. Each State determines for itself the measure of naval strength which it judges to be necessary to its security. No State expects to have to encounter the whole world in arms or makes its provision in view of any such chimerical contingency. The utmost that any State can do is to adjust its naval

I

policy to a rational estimate of all the reasonably probable contingencies of international conflict, due regard being had to the extent of its financial resources and to such other requirements of national defence as circumstances impose on it. Germany, for example, has proclaimed to all the world in the preamble to the Navy Law of 1900 that—

" In order to protect German trade and commerce under existing conditions, only one thing will suffice, namely, Germany must possess a battle fleet of such strength that even for the most powerful naval adversary a war would involve such risks as to make that Power's own supremacy doubtful. For this purpose it is not absolutely necessary that the German fleet should be as strong as that of the greatest naval Power, for, as a rule, a great naval Power will not be in a position to concentrate all its forces against us."

I am not concerned in any way with the political aspects of this memorable declaration. But its bearing on the naval policy of the British Empire is manifest and direct. England is beyond all question " the greatest naval Power " in the world. The declaration of Germany thus lays upon England the indefeasible obligation of taking care that by no efforts of any other Power shall her " own supremacy" —that is her capacity to secure and maintain the command of the sea in all reasonably probable

contingencies of international conflict—be rendered
doubtful. There is no State in the world on which
decisive defeat at sea would inflict such irretrievable
disaster as it would on England and her Empire.
These islands would be open to invasion—and
if to invasion to conquest and subjugation—the
commerce of the whole Empire would be annihilated,
and the Empire itself would be dismembered. I
need not attempt to determine what measure of
naval strength is required to avert this unspeak-
able calamity. It suffices to say that whatever the
measure may be it must be provided and maintained at all hazards. That is merely the axiomatic
expression of the things that belong to our peace.

It will be observed that the German declaration
assumes that " a great naval Power will not, as a
rule, be in a position to concentrate all its forces
against " a single adversary. This raises at once the
question of the distribution of naval force, or of
what has been called the peace strategy of position.
I shall endeavour to discuss the problem with as
little reference as may be to an actual state of war
between any two individual and specific naval
Powers. I shall merely assume that of two possible
belligerents one is so far stronger than the other as
to look with confidence to being able in the event
of war to secure and maintain its own command of
the sea ; and in order not to complicate the problem

unduly I shall include in the term "belligerent" not merely a single Power but an alliance of one or more separate Powers, while still adhering to the assumption that the relative strength of the two belligerents is as defined above. If England is one of the Powers affected it is manifest from what has already been said that this assumption is a legitimate one.

In such a situation it stands to reason that the concentration of the whole force of the stronger belligerent against the whole force equally concentrated of the weaker belligerent would not be necessary and would very rarely be expedient. The stronger belligerent would of course seek, in time of war, so to dispose his forces as to make it impossible for the weaker fleets of his adversary to take the sea without being brought to a decisive action, and he would so order his peace strategy of position as to further that paramount purpose. But it does not follow that being superior in the measure above defined he would need to concentrate all his available forces for that purpose. He would concentrate so much of his forces as would ensure victory in the encounters anticipated—so far as mere numbers apart from fighting efficiency can ensure victory—and the residue would be available for other and subsidiary purposes. If there were no residue, then the required superiority would not have been attained, and the belligerent who has neglected to attain it must take the consequences. One of these consequences would certainly be that the other and subsidiary purposes above mentioned would have to be neglected until the main issue was decided, and if these purposes were of any moment he would have so far to pay the penalty of his neglect. Nothing is more fatal in warfare than to attempt to be equally strong everywhere. If you cannot do everything you desire at once you must concentrate all your energies on doing the most important and the most vital things first. When the tree is cut down the branches will fall of themselves. The history of the War of American Independence is full of illustrations of the neglect of this paramount principle. England was worsted much more by faulty distribution than by insufficiency of force.

At the same time it must be observed that the outlying and subsidiary purposes of the conflict cannot be of vital moment so long as the superior belligerent is at firm grips with the central forces of his adversary. We are dealing with the assumption that of two belligerents one is so far superior to the other that he may entertain a reasonable confidence of being able to deny the command of the sea to his adversary and in the end to secure it for himself. It is an essential part of this assumption

that the forces of the superior belligerent will be
so disposed as to make it exceedingly difficult
and, subject to the fortune of war, practically impossible for any considerable portion of the enemy's
forces to act on a vigorous offensive without being
speedily brought to book by a superior force of his
adversary, and that the peace strategy of the latter
will have been ordered to that end.   So long as this
is the case the virtual command of the sea will be
in the hands of the superior belligerent, even though
his forces may be so concentrated, in accordance
with the dispositions of the enemy, as to leave many
regions of the sea apparently unguarded.   They are
adequately guarded by the fact that the enemy is
ex hypothesi unable to reach them—or if by a successful evasion of his adversary's guard he manages to
send a detachment, large or small, to aim at some
outlying objective, the initial superiority of force
possessed by his adversary will always enable the
latter to send a superior force in pursuit of the
fugitive.   Much harm may be done before the
fugitive is brought to book, but no State, however
strong, need ever expect to go to war without running risks and suffering occasional and partial
reverses.

It is thus a pure delusion to assume, as loose
thinkers on the subject too often assume, that the
command of the sea must be either surrendered or

imperilled by a superior belligerent who, apparently
neglecting those regions of the sea which are not
immediately assailed or threatened, concentrates
his forces in the positions best calculated to enable
him to get the better of his adversary, or who in
time of peace so orders his strategy of position as
to secure that advantage at once should war un-
happily break out. Not long ago the Leader o
the Opposition in the House of Commons used the
following words :—" Ten years ago we not only had
the command of the sea, but we had the command
of every sea. We have the command of no sea in
the world except the North Sea at this moment."
Those who have followed and assimilated the exposition of the true meaning of the command of
the sea given in these pages will readily discern
how mischievous a travesty of that meaning is contained in these words. There is, as I have shown,
no such thing as a command of the sea in time of
peace. The phrase is merely a definition of the
paramount objective of naval warfare as such. Ten
years ago we had no command of any sea because
we were not at war with any naval Power. The
concentration of a large portion of our naval forces
in the North Sea is no surrender of our command of
the sea in any part of the world, because that command does not exist, never has existed in time of
peace, and never can exist even in time of war until

we have fought for it and secured it. The concentration in question is, together with the simultaneous disposition of the residue of our naval forces in different parts of the world, merely the expression of that peace strategy of position which, in the judgment of those who are responsible for it, is best calculated in the more probable, yet possibly quite remote, contingencies of international conflict, to enable our fleets to get the better of our enemies and thereby ultimately to secure the command of the sea in any and every part of the world in which we have maritime interests to defend. There are, it is true, some disadvantages involved in a close and sustained concentration of naval forces, especially in home waters. Naval officers lose in breadth and variety of experience and in the self-reliance which comes of independent command, while the prestige of the flag is in some measure diminished by the infrequency of its appearance in distant seas. But these, after all, are subsidiary considerations which must be subordinated to the paramount needs of a sound strategy, whether offensive or defensive.

It follows from the foregoing exposition of the principles which govern the strategic distribution of naval force in peace and war that a great naval Power must often maintain fleets of considerable strength in distant seas. England has for many generations maintained such a fleet in the Medi-

terranean, and it is hard to see how any reasonably probable change in the international situation
could absolve her from that obligation.   There are
other and more distant stations on which she has
maintained and still does maintain squadrons in a
strength which has varied greatly from time to time
in accordance with the changing phases of international relations and of strategic requirements as
affected thereby.   The measure of these requirements is determined from time to time by the known
strength of the hostile forces which would have to
be encountered in any reasonably probable contingencies of international conflict.   But there is
one antecedent requirement which is common to
all considerable detachments of naval force in distant waters.   In order to maintain their efficiency
and mobility they must have a naval base conveniently situated within the limits of their station
to which they may resort from time to time for
repair, refit, and supply.   The need for supply at
the base is less paramount than that for refit and
repair, because it is manifest that the control of
maritime communications which has enabled the
requisite stores to reach the base will also enable
them to reach the ships themselves, wherever they
may be at the moment.   But for all refit and repair
which cannot be effected by the ships' companies
themselves, with the aid of an attached repair ship,

the ships must go to the base, and that base must be furnished with docks capable of receiving them.

It is essential to note that the base is there for the sake of the ships. The ships are not there for the sake of the base. It is a fatal inversion of all sound principles of naval strategy to suppose that the ships owe, or can afford, to the base any other form of defence than that which is inherent in their paramount and primary task of controlling the maritime communications which lead to it. So long as they can do this the base will be exposed only to such attacks as can be delivered by a force which has evaded but not defeated the naval guard, and to this extent the base must be fortified and garrisoned ; for, of course, if the naval guard has been decisively defeated, the control of maritime communications has passed into the hands of the enemy, and nothing but the advance of a relieving naval force, too strong for the enemy to resist, can prevent the base being invested from the sea and utlimately reduced. It will be seen from this how absurd it is ever to speak of a naval base as commanding the adjacent seas. As such it does not command, and never can command, any portion of the sea which lies beyond the range of its own guns. All that it ever does or can do is, by its resources for repair, refit, and supply, to enable the fleet based upon it constantly to renew its efficiency and mobility, and thereby to discharge its appointed task of controlling the maritime communications entrusted to its keeping. But such command is in all cases exercised by the fleet and not by the base. If the fleet is not there or not equal to its task, the mere possession of the base is nearly always a source of weakness and not of strength to the naval Power which holds it.

It is held by some that the occupation of naval bases in distant seas by a Power which is not strong enough to make sure of controlling the maritime communications which alone give to such bases their strategic value and importance is a great advantage to such a Power and a corresponding disadvantage to all its possible adversaries in war. It will readily be seen from what has been said that this is in large measure a delusion. As against a weaker adversary than itself the occupation of such bases may be an appreciable advantage to the Power which holds them, but only if the adversary in question has in the waters affected interests which are too important to be sacrificed without a struggle. On the other hand, as against an adversary strong enough to secure the command of the sea and determined to hold it at all hazards, the occupation of such distant bases can very rarely be of any advantage to the weaker belligerent and may very often expose him to reverses which, if not positively disastrous, must always be exceedingly mortifying. Of two things one. Either the belligerent in such a plight must detach a naval force sufficient to cover the outlying base, and thus, by dispersing naval forces which he desired to keep concentrated, he must expose his detachment to destruction by a stronger force of the enemy, or he must leave the base to its fate, in which case it is certain to fall in the long run. In point of fact the occupation of distant bases by any naval Power is merely the giving of hostages to any and every other Power which in the day of conflict can establish its command of the sea. That is the plain philosophy of the whole question.

It only remains to consider very briefly the question of the supply of fleets operating in distant waters. In a very interesting and suggestive paper on the " Supply and Communications of a Fleet," Admiral Sir Cyprian Bridge has pointed out that " in time of peace as well as in time of war there is a continuous consumption of the articles of various kinds used on board ship, viz., naval stores, ordnance stores, engineers' stores, victualling stores, coal, water, etc." Of these the consumption of victualling stores is alone constant, being determined by the number of men to be victualled from day to day. The consumption of nearly all the other stores will vary greatly according as the ship is more or less at sea, and it is safe to say that for a given number of ships the consumption will be much greater in time of war, especially in coal, engineers' stores, and ordnance stores, than it is in time of peace. But in peace conditions Admiral Bridge estimated that for a fleet consisting of four battleships, four large cruisers, four second-class cruisers, thirteen smaller vessels of various kinds, and three torpedo craft, together with their auxiliaries, the *minimum* requirements for six months—assuming that the ships started with full supplies, and that they returned to their principal base at the end of the period—would be about 6750 tons of stores and ammunition, and 46,000 tons of coal, without including fresh water. The requirements of water would not be less than 30,000 tons in the six months, and of this the ships could distil about half without greatly increasing their coal consumption ; the remainder, some 15,000 or 16,000 tons, would have to be brought to them. In time of war the requirements of coal would probably be nearly three times as great as in time of peace, and the requirements of ammunition—estimated in time of peace at 1140 tons—might easily be ten times as great. Thus in addition to the foregoing figures we have 16,000 tons of water, and in war time a further *minimum* addition of some 90,000 tons of coal and 10,260 tons of ammunition, making in all a round total of 170,000 tons for a fleet of the size specified, which was approximately the strength of the China Fleet, under the command of Admiral Bridge, at the time when his paper was written.

All these supplies have to be delivered or obtained periodically and at convenient intervals in the course of every six months. They are supplies which the ships must obtain as often as they want them without necessarily going back to their principal base for the purpose, and even the principal base must obtain them periodically from the home sources of supply. There are two alternative ways of maintaining this continuous stream of supply. One is that in advance of the principal base, what is called a secondary base should be established from which the ships can obtain the stores required, a continuous stream of transports bringing the stores required to the secondary base from sources farther afield, either from the principal base or from the home sources of supply. The other method is to have no secondary base—which, since it contains indispensable stores, must be furnished with some measure of local defence, and which, as a place of storage, may turn out to be in quite the wrong place for the particular operations in hand—but to seize and occupy a "flying base," neither permanent nor designated beforehand, but selected for the occasion according to the exigencies of the strategic situation, and capable of being shifted at will in response to any change in those exigencies. History shows that the latter method has been something like the normal procedure in war alike in times past and in the present day. The alternative method is perhaps rather adapted to the convenience of peace conditions than to the exigencies of war requirements. During his watch on Toulon Nelson established a flying base at Maddalena Bay, in Sardinia, and very rarely used the more distant permanent base at Gibraltar. Togo, as I have stated in an earlier chapter, established a flying base first at the Elliot Islands and afterwards at Dalny, during the war in the Far East. Instances might easily be multiplied to show in which direction the experience of war points, and how far that direction has been deflected by the possibly deceptive teaching of peace. I shall not, however, presume to pronounce *ex cathedrâ* between two alternative methods each of which is sanctioned by high naval authority. I will only remark in conclusion that though the establishment of permanent secondary bases may, in certain exceptional cases, be defensible and even expedient, yet their multiplication, beyond such exceptional cases of proved and acknowledged expediency, is very greatly to be deprecated. The old rule applies—*Entia non sunt præter necessitatem multiplicanda.*

My task is now finished—I will not say completed, for the subject of naval warfare is far too vast to be exhausted within the narrow compass of a Manual. I should hardly exaggerate if I said that nearly every paragraph I have written might be expanded into a chapter, and every chapter into a volume, and that even so the subject would not be exhausted. All I have endeavoured to do is to expound briefly and in simple language the nature of naval warfare, its inherent limitations as an agency for subduing an enemy's will, the fundamental principles which underlie its methods, and the concrete problems which the application of those methods presents. Tactical questions I have not touched at all ; strategic questions only incidentally, and so far as they were implicated in the discussion of methods. Political issues and questions of international policy I have eschewed as far as might be, and so far as it was necessary to deal with them I have endeavoured to do so in broad and abstract terms. Of the many shortcomings in my handling of the subject no one can be more conscious than I am myself. Yet I must anticipate one criticism which is not unlikely to be made, and that is that I have repeated and insisted on certain phrases and ideas such as " command of the sea," " control of maritime communications," " the fleet in being," " blockade," and the like, until they might almost be regarded as an obsession. Rightly or wrongly that has, at any rate, been done of deliberate intent. The phrases in question are in all men's mouths. The ideas they stand for are constantly misunderstood, misinterpreted, and misapplied. I hold that, rightly understood, they embody the whole philosophy of naval warfare. I have therefore lost no opportunity of insisting on them, knowing full well that it is only by frequent iteration that sound ideas can be implanted in minds not attuned to their reception.

INDEX

147